ENGLISH ✛ HERITAGE

Book of
Stone Age Britain

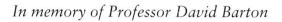

In memory of Professor David Barton

ENGLISH ⌗ HERITAGE

Book of
Stone Age
Britain

Nicholas Barton

B. T. Batsford / English Heritage
London

Typeset by Bernard Cavender Design & Greenwood Graphics Publishing
Printed and bound in Great Britain by The Bath Press, Bath

Published by B.T. Batsford Ltd
583 Fulham Road, London SW6 5BY

A CIP catalogue record for this book is
available from the British Library

ISBN 0 7134 6800 9 (cased)
0 7134 6846 7 (limp)

(Front) Selected artefacts, human remains and
fauna from the Late Upper Palaeolithic site of Gough's
Cave, Cheddar Gorge, Somerset (Photo: Frank Greenway).

(Back) Ovate handaxe from Boxgrove
(Photo: John Mitchell).

Contents

Illustrations

Colour plates

List of tables

Acknowledgements

A large number of people have contributed either directly or indirectly towards the writing of this book. I owe a considerable debt of gratitude to my friends and colleagues who painstakingly read through early drafts of chapters and endured a constant hail of e-mail and telephone enquiries. In particular I would like to thank my wife Alison Roberts, Peter Mitchell, Chris Stringer, Andy Currant, Stephen Aldhouse-Green, Simon Lewis, Nick Ashton and several of my past students in Oxford for their comments which were mercifully restrained and always constructive. I would like also to pay particular homage to my father, David Barton, who was one of my main inspirations for embarking on archaeology. He read with enthusiasm some of the earlier versions of chapters but sadly died a few months before the book was completed.

I owe a great deal to staff and colleagues at Oxford Brookes University who helped in the production of this book. In particular, I would like to warmly thank Lisa Hill and Bob Pomfret (Educational Media Unit) for their patience and constant good humour and Gerry Black (Social Sciences) for her calm fortitude in the face of the continuous demands on her time. Between them they expertly created or redrew figures 2 and 9 (after Tixier), 10 and 13 (after Bordes), 15 (after Stringer and Gamble), 16 (after Dansgaard), 17 (after Woillard and Mook), 18 (after Broeker and Denton), 19 (after Zahn), 20 (after Patience and Kroon), 21 (after Bowen, Rose and others), 24 and 25 (after Van Andel), 29, 30, 33 and 98 (after Evans), 40, 53 and 62 (after Mithen), 67

(after Tyldesley and Roe), 70 (after Boule), 77 (after Plisson and Geneste), 79 (after Klíma), 81 (after Lawson), 82 (after Mellars), 83 and 88 and 99–100 (after Jacobi), 89–90 and 105 (after Adams), 91 (after Lowe and others) 107 and 111. The following photographs were also reproduced by them: 5 and 71 (after Bordes), 61 (First Europeans Exhibition), 72 (after Bräuer), 78 (after Novosti), 109 (after Rust) and 14.

The following people or institutions must be thanked for their illustrations. Hazel Martingell drew 3, 4, 7, 11, 22, 23, 26, 27, 43, 75, 76, 84, 92, 101, 102. John Lord supplied 1 and 12. Permission to reproduce 6, 14, 28, 59 and colour plate 3 was kindly given by Ian Tattersall. John Wymer allowed the use of 8, as did Stephen Mithen of 53 and 62, and Peter Berridge supplied 32 and 74. Chris Stringer supplied 31, 37, 38, 56, 58, 60, 63, 64, 65, 68, 69, 73, 94, 95, 96 and colour plate 4. The frontcover was photographed by Frank Greenaway. Illustrations 34, 35, 54, 55 (drawn by Phil Dean), 103, 112, 113 and colour plates 5 and 8 were provided by Jill Cook and Nick Ashton. The Boxgrove Project (Mark Roberts and Simon Parfitt) supplied 36, 41, 42, 49 (drawn by Julian Cross), 50 (drawn by Simon James) and 51. John Mitchell made available 44 (drawn by Geoff Wallis), 52, colour plate 6 and the back cover photograph. Elizabeth Walker supplied 66, 85, 86 and 87. Figures 39, 57 and 80 were reproduced courtesy of Thessaloniki Museum, Erkrath Museum and Ulm Museum, respectively. Alison Roberts supplied 97 (drawn by Karen Hughes) and Klaus Bokelmann photographed 110. The author would also like to acknowledge the drawings of Christine Wilson (106) and Geoff Wallis (108). Hartmüt Thieme supplied **colour plate 7**, while Brian Chambers and Nigel Mills gave permission to reproduce **colour plate 16**. The other colour plates were made available by the following: (**11**) Philip Powell, (**13**) Cath Price and (**15**) Andrew David. Photographs for **45, 46, 47, 48, 93** and **colour plates 1, 2, 9, 10** and **12** were taken by myself.

Various institutions retain the copyright of illustrations reproduced in this book. They include the Natural History Museum (**37, 38,** **63, 65, 68, 69, 94, 95, 96** and **colour plate 4**), Thames and Hudson (**56, 60, 64, 53** and **62**), the British Museum (**34, 35, 55, 97, 103, 112, 113** and **colour plates 5** and **8**), the National Museum of Wales (**66, 85, 86** and **87**) and the University Museum, Oxford (**colour plate 11**).

Finally I would like to acknowledge Stephen Johnson, the editor of the series, for inviting me to write this book, and Monica Kendall of Batsford for guiding it through to the finished product, Anne Dunbar-Nobes for editing the book, and Susanne Atkin for the index.

Introduction

Just over 200 years ago, on 22 June 1797, John Frere read a short paper entitled (an) 'Account of Flint Weapons discovered at Hoxne in Suffolk' to a distinguished gathering of the Society of Antiquaries of London. At the time no one realized that it was a major landmark in the development of prehistory. In it he referred to flint tools found in undisturbed geological deposits near the base of a clay brickpit at Hoxne in Suffolk. With breathtaking audacity, he also announced that they were made by pre-metal-using societies who occupied 'a very remote period indeed; even beyond that of the present world', by implication extending further back in time than either the ancient Greeks or Romans. Mr Frere was warmly thanked for his 'curious and most interesting communication' but his comments were soon forgotten.

Today, most of us take for granted Frere's remarkably perceptive ideas. The term 'Stone Age' was popularized in the nineteenth century (with the publication in 1836 of C. J. Thomsen's *Three Age System*) and subsequently further sub-divisions – Palaeolithic, Mesolithic and Neolithic – were added to account for successive tool-using cultures. This book is about the earliest of these divisions: the Palaeolithic or Old Stone Age. It begins with the first recognizable stone tools, around 2.5 million years ago (in Africa), and continues up until the latest Palaeolithic occurrences in Europe about 10,000 years ago.

One of the enormous attractions of the Palaeolithic is that it cross-cuts a range of disciplines as diverse as climatology, sedimentology, pollen analysis, palaeontology, anthropology and archaeology. It is also a subject which is advancing rapidly; virtually every day new sites and fossils are discovered that form the basis of fresh ideas which constantly challenge, reshape and update our views of the past. This book represents an attempt to summarize some of the most recent discoveries which have appeared in the scientific literature, and to integrate them with longer held ideas about our past. Within this broad scope, I have tried to address some of the main themes of human biological and behavioural change through time, and especially the relationships between the two. The principal geographic subject area is Britain, but inevitably I have strayed beyond the geopolitical confines of these islands, confines which are, in any case, largely meaningless from a Palaeolithic point of view. In the same context, most of the book concerns England and Wales. Scotland and Ireland receive scarce mention due mainly to the fact that very little evidence of Palaeolithic occupation has been forthcoming from Scotland, and, up until now, none at all from Ireland. The timescales referred to in the text are broadly geological ones. Except for radiocarbon ages which are expressed in years bp (before present, conventionally placed at AD 1950) precise calendar dates have been avoided wherever possible. This is partly to simplify matters and also because it reflects the current lack of high resolution dating for the majority of the Palaeolithic.

Among the most challenging aspects of writing a book of this kind is the enormous wealth of new literature that continues to appear on the subject. Many of the ideas expressed here will therefore inevitably require modifying in the light of fresh developments over the coming months and years. Related to this point is acknowledgement of the fact that there is rarely ever one simple view on any topic. To counter this I have tried wherever possible to represent the different sides of the arguments, but naturally I have incorporated my own biases. Archaeology is often about controversy and disagreement of interpretation; I hope some of the flavour of these debates will be brought out in the following pages.

1
Stone tools and toolmaking

An apt description of archaeology is the study of our human past through its surviving material traces. For the 'Palaeolithic' or 'Old Stone Age' the most durable remains are stone artefacts which, unlike organic substances of wood, bone, ivory, antler and so forth, are virtually indestructible. Thus, it is a sobering thought that for about 99 per cent of human history, the most enduring – and sometimes the only – evidence of human activities comes from stone tools. To say that this presents a considerable intellectual challenge is no doubt an understatement, but in the following chapters we shall see how, by combining various disciplinary approaches, stone artefacts can act as rich sources of information about our human past. Among other things we shall consider the function of stone tools, the manner in which they were made and used, and how by studying their forms and archaeological context, more complex issues can be addressed, such as how lifestyles changed through time and how we can enter into the minds of the people themselves. To begin with, however, we need to consider some of the first principles of technology and the overall time framework in which stone artefacts are situated.

Stone technology

Various ways of looking at technology are routinely employed by Palaeolithic archaeologists. These range from experimental duplication of stone tools to refitting studies in which component artefacts are literally pieced together in a three-dimensional jigsaw puzzle (**colour plates 1** and **2**). Another leading contribution comes from microwear analysis which enables the function of stone tools to be accurately determined by examining microscopically the surfaces of artefacts for polishes and other use-wear traces (see **52**).

One of the most direct methods of studying artefacts is still experimental flintknapping. The term 'knapping' comes from the Dutch word meaning to flake, snap or break and refers to the methods of percussion and pressure that are used in the manufacture of stone tools. Today, the leading British exponent of this craft is John Lord, who lives near Brandon, Norfolk (**1**). Although almost entirely self-taught, Lord relies on traditional methods passed down by generations of Brandon flintknappers who earned a living by manufacturing gunflints for flintlock rifles.

A vital first lesson, as Lord reveals, is in identifying and selecting suitable stone for flaking. In southern Britain, the most appropriate rock-types available are chert and flint (a finer-grained type of chert). Both of them are tough but relatively brittle, which makes them ideally suited for flaking purposes. Despite this fragility, the edges of a freshly struck flint are so sharp that they compare favourably with surgical steel. The distinctive conchoidal (shell-like) patterns left by flaking also make it relatively easy for archaeologists to distinguish intentional

manufacture from accidental breaks caused by frost cracking or other natural damage. Elsewhere in Britain, where flint is scarcer, alternative sources of workable stone are provided by quartzite, volcanic tuffs and metamorphic sandstones. In more recent prehistory, rocks like these were sometimes deliberately chosen for their hardness, rather than their sharp, brittle qualities. Instead of flaking them, they were often fashioned into tools by pecking and polishing. Lastly, it may be surprising to learn that selecting the right rock often depends as much on a well-tuned ear as on a specialist eye! A light tap on the surface of flint can reveal much about its internal consistency. A clear bell-like ring normally means the flint is free from internal flaws and will therefore be good for

1 John Lord, flint mastercraftsman, demonstrating knapping by direct percussion using an antler billet.

2 Two reduction sequences (*chaînes opératoires*) from raw material to finished implements. Left: the manufacture of a handaxe. Right: the production of blades and blade tools. Each sequence requires a very different approach to the raw material and results in distinctive by-products.

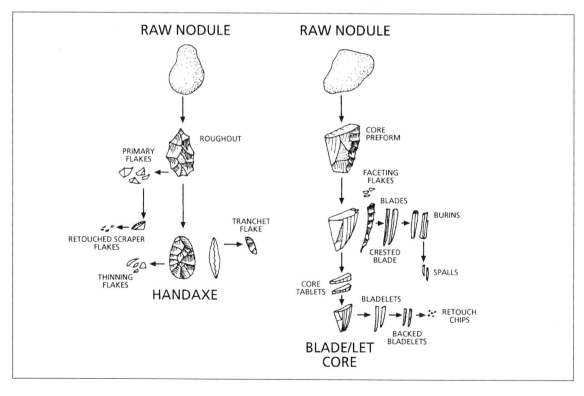

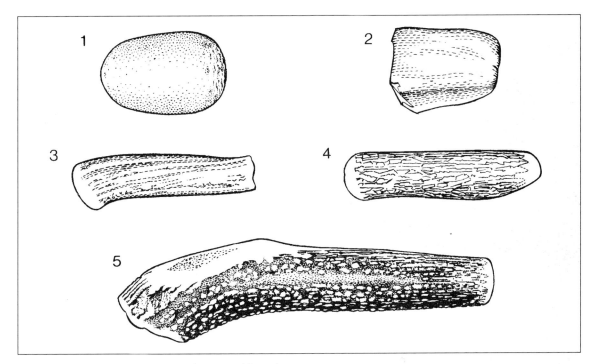

flaking. Interestingly, an expert knapper like John Lord also relies on colour as an indicator of quality, suggesting that even the aesthetic appeal of stone may have a practical basis.

Some of the finest flint for knapping can be mined directly from chalk. While the best sources are usually underground, flint can also be quarried from eroding surface exposures, such as sea cliffs. In these cases the flint nodules often have a thick chalky-white outer skin, commonly referred to as cortex. Secondary sources of flint, such as those redeposited in river gravels, beaches or in glacial outwash sediments, are less predictable for flaking, but were extensively exploited in the past because of their abundance. In rocks like these, the physical weathering generally leaves a thinner, sometimes battered cortex, which is quite distinguishable. The sourcing of raw materials in relation to Palaeolithic sites has important implications for studying past behaviours.

The flintknapping process involves reducing the rock to its required shape with the help of a percussor. Familiarity with each of the steps in the reduction process and the resulting by-products are important because they enable the

3 John Lord's flintknapping toolkit. 1 quartzite hammerstone, 2 sandstone abrader, 3 small antler hammer, 4 antler punch, 5 antler hammer.

archaeologist to identify the nature of tool-making activities, even if the final products themselves are missing. To begin with, knapping requires a reasonable degree of hand–eye coordination in first finding a suitably acute angle on the rock (nodule) and then striking a glancing blow using a hammerstone. Apart from the simplest technologies, where there is only minimal modification, reduction normally involves the removal of many successive flakes. Various inferences can be drawn from knapping. For example, long and complicated sequences need to be learned; they also imply certain cognitive abilities on the part of the toolmaker, as in being able to mentally visualize the end-product. This is as true in making a single tool, like a handaxe, as in preparing slender blades for tool production. Examples of two reduction sequences and their typical by-products are illustrated here (**2**).

For today's flintknappers like John Lord a variety of hammer types (**3**) are employed in the different stages of reduction. For example, in the

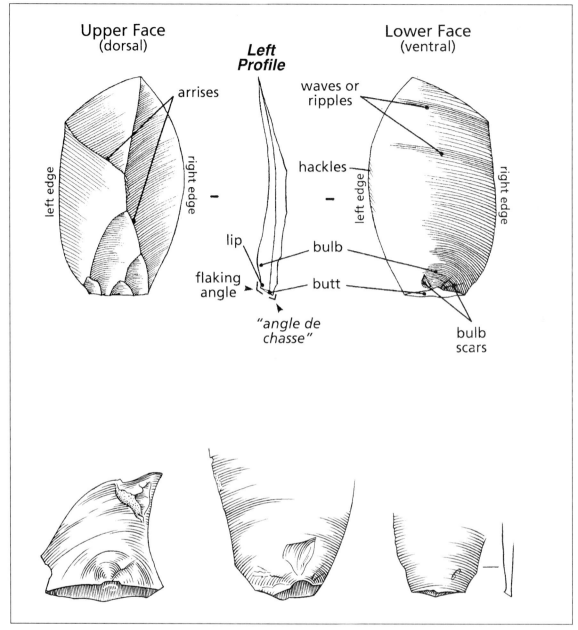

4 Diagnostic features of knapped flakes. Different hammer types leave distinctive characteristics. Left: hard stone – large butt, pronounced bulb, cones visible on the butt, percussion rings on bulb. Centre: soft stone – large butt, flattish bulb, bulbar scar originating from butt, many small fissures radiating from butt, slight lipping between butt and bulb, percussion rings towards butt end. Right: antler – weak bulb, small butt, bulbar scar away from butt, few percussion rings, pronounced lipping.

early stages when larger, thicker flakes are detached he generally employs a dense stone hammer (quartzite). In the later stages for the more delicate tasks of thinning and finishing he graduates to lighter deer antler hammers or those made of softer stone (e.g. limestone). Diagnostic features on the artefacts often allow the technologist to determine which of the hammer types was used in the past and this can be helpful in distinguishing certain industries (4). Direct

5 Upper Palaeolithic reindeer antler hammer from Laugerie Haute-Ouest, south-west France. The hammer head shows percussive damage, and small flint chips, detached during knapping, are also embedded in this end.

evidence for stone percussors of quartzite and other hard rocks is generally fairly common in the archaeological record as they can be recognized by their heavily battered exteriors. On the other hand, organic hammers or ones made of softer stone are much less likely to survive because of their friability. Nevertheless, their presence in the past is confirmed by very exceptional examples like the 500,000-year-old hammers of antler and bone from Boxgrove (see **49**). The strength and flexibility of antler makes it ideal for detaching long, wafer-thin flakes and these tools are believed to have been used in finishing handaxes and other bifacial implements (**5** and **colour plate** 3).

Stone artefacts as cultural markers

For convenience, the Palaeolithic is sub-divided typologically according to the presence of certain tools and distinctive modes of tool manufacture. The various typological phases are not strictly defined in chronological terms but are ordered in a relative sense. This slight fuzziness allows for an overlap in time to exist between the different phases either locally or at a wider geographical scale. The basic idea behind the classification is that tools are made in accordance with a persistent cultural tradition which was sometimes extremely longlasting. The scheme is also based on the general premise of technological progression.

The most universally accepted typology is still that proposed by Grahame Clark, with a four-fold division of the early Stone Age (**6**). Each of the divisions (modes) is characterized by a broad technological standardization of stone artefacts, and allows for some internal variation within each of the modes.

Mode 1: Oldowan

The earliest stone tools yet found date back more than 2.5 million years. They come from Ethiopia, east and southern Africa and consist of simple flakes and flaked pebble tools (**7**). The hominids who made them (see Chapter 2) had mastered the idea of finding acute angles on pebbles, in order to provide a suitable striking platform for removing flakes. The flakes were

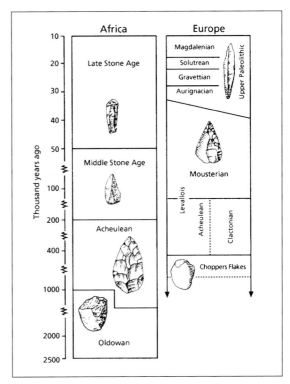

6 Timeline comparing the Palaeolithic sequences in Europe and Africa.

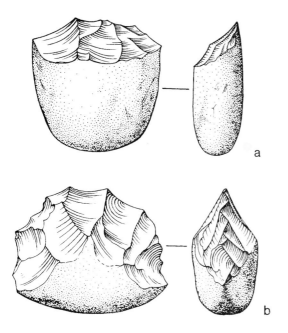

7 Mode 1 Oldowan pebble chopping tools. a) Unifacial (one-sided) tool, b) bifacial (dual-sided).

struck with a hard hammerstone using a direct percussive technique. Flakes made in this way have a pronounced bulb of percussion, often with conchoidal rings on the bulb itself (see **4**). The aim of the earliest toolmaking was to produce flakes with razor-sharp edges for cutting purposes. The cores may also have acted as tools as they too had acute edges formed by negative flake scars. The cores are sometimes referred to as choppers or chopping-tools if they are flaked on both sides to form an acute edge.

Although there is no compelling evidence of anything as early as the Oldowan in Britain or Europe, some of the oldest industries do contain simple choppers and flake tools. In Britain these are generally referred to as the Clactonian, after finds in ancient river channel deposits at the Essex seaside resort. Not everyone agrees with this view, however. Some Palaeolithic specialists believe that the manufacture of British pebble tools may simply reflect expedient use of locally available raw materials, because pebble tools do occasionally turn up in later prehistoric industries as well. In these cases they are

definitely not part of a Clactonian cultural tradition but seem to be a response to the limited choice in flakeable stone. We shall return to the Clactonian in Chapter 4.

Mode 2: Acheulian

The appearance of more elaborate bifacial tools called handaxes is signalled in the African archaeological record from about 1.4 million years ago. They were primarily made by early hominids of the genus *Homo* who later spread out into many parts of the Old World. Artefacts of this kind were first described from a quarry near St Acheul, northern France, which then gave its name to the cultural tradition. The basic teardrop shape of handaxes is remarkably consistent throughout the whole of their geographical distribution, which stretches from China and the Far East to western Europe and as far south as southern Africa. They have also been discovered in a variety of palaeo-environments. The tools are usually highly symmetrical (**8**). Compared to a simple chopping tool, the cutting edge was greatly increased by flaking around the whole of the perimeter.

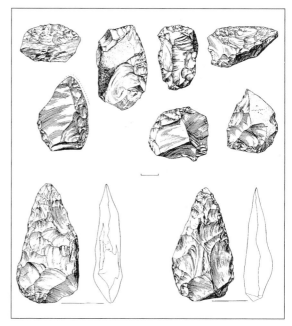

8 Mode 2 Acheulian scrapers (above) and pointed handaxes (below). 2-cm scale bar.

The process of manufacturing a handaxe was much more complicated than making a pebble tool. It involved a longer sequence of steps beginning with initial shaping of a nodule (using a hard hammer), sometimes followed by thinning in which a soft hammer (e.g. wood, antler, bone) was used (see **3**). The finishing touches sometimes included the removal of tranchet flakes to produce a wafer-thin cutting edge at one end (see **2** and **46**). Making a handaxe therefore entails a greater degree of skill and a use of memory well beyond the capability of non-human primates. Thus, it is justly seen as a major technological breakthrough, revealing a significant leap forward in increased human brain function.

The earliest British examples of handaxes are from sites like Boxgrove, dating to over 500,000 years ago. Here they have been found in association with large animals like horse and rhinoceros and there is good reason for seeing them as all-purpose butchery tools. The Acheulian also includes other flaked tools such as scrapers (**8**), but at Boxgrove the latter only account for a small proportion of tool finds. Both mode 1 and mode 2 industries are synonymous with the Lower Palaeolithic era.

Mode 3: Mousterian

The Mousterian, named after the Le Moustier rockshelters in south-west France, is a Middle Palaeolithic technology dominated by flakes, including retouched tools made on flakes. In Europe and western Asia the Mousterian appeared around 200,000 years ago and overlapped with the Acheulian for thousands of years. In Europe the Mousterian is generally associated with Neanderthals (*Homo neanderthalensis*), though in the Near East it occurs in both Neanderthal and modern human (*Homo sapiens sapiens*) contexts. The latest Mousterian occurrences in Europe are at sites such as Zafarraya in southern Spain (30,000 bp) where they are linked with Neanderthal activities.

Among the distinctive hallmarks of the Mousterian is the increased reliance on a new technique for making stone flakes of pre-determined size and thickness. This technique is termed 'Levallois', after the Paris suburb where it was first recognized (**9**). The aim of the method was the production of one or several successive flakes whose oval 'tortoise' shape had been precisely controlled by the maker. The whole sequence could be executed using hard hammer percussion (see **4**). A related technique involved preparatory flaking from one or both ends of the core resulting in triangular flakes used in making Mousterian points (**9** and **10**).

It is essential to point out that the Levallois technique also appears in some mode 2 Acheulian assemblages and is thus only one of a number of relevant factors in identifying the Mousterian. The full criteria for analyzing Mousterian assemblages owe much to the analytical methods and typology of the famous French archaeologist François Bordes. According to his scheme the Mousterian can be sub-divided into five variants: Typical, Ferrassie, Quina, Denticulate and Mousterian of Acheulian Tradition (MAT) (**Table 1** and **10**).

Using Bordes' classification it is possible to describe most of the British examples as being of MAT-type with flat-based, cordate handaxes (see **colour plate 8**) and their waste products. Based on French parallels and the limited chronological evidence available the MAT findspots would appear to date to a period in the last glaciation (60,000–35,000 bp).

Mode 4: Upper Palaeolithic

This technology appeared abruptly in Europe at around 40,000 years ago and remained in use until 10,000 bp. The Upper Palaeolithic is only found in association with *Homo sapiens sapiens* and, because it signals a distinct technological break with the past, it is believed to have been introduced by new incoming populations to Europe. The industry is characterized by narrow blades struck from cores (see **colour plate 2**). These artefacts (whose length is more than twice their width) had numerous advantages: their standardized shape meant that they could be

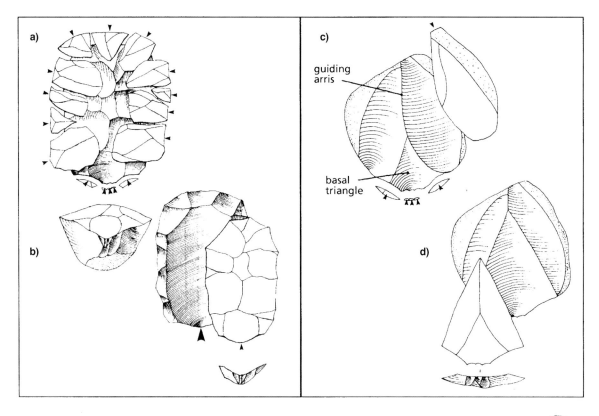

9 Left: 'Classic' Levallois core technique. a) The nodule is prepared so as to have two slightly domed surfaces, a continuous striking platform is prepared around the circumference of the core and the upper face is carefully shaped by centripetal removals; b) The Levallois flake is struck from a prepared platform at one end of the core. Right: Multiple flake Levallois technique for making points. c) Preparatory flaking from one or both ends of the core; d) striking flakes with a more elongated or triangular form.

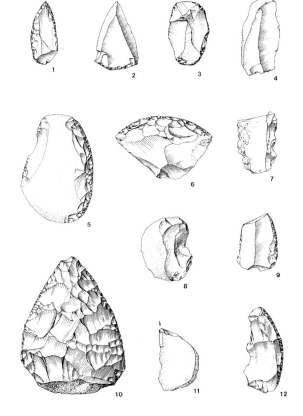

10 Mode 3 Mousterian industry. Selected tools: 1 Mousterian point, 2 Levallois point, 3 backed knife, 4 naturally backed knife, 5 convex side-scraper, 6 transverse scraper (Quina type), 7 denticulate, 8 notch, 9 side-scraper, 10 flat-based (bout coupé) handaxe, 11 burin, 12 convex side-scraper.

Table 1

Bordes' five Mousterian variants based on a type-list of 63 different tools.
The tools were also grouped into four main sub-categories: I – Levallois flakes and points;
II – various side-scrapers; III – backed knives and Upper Palaeolithic-type tools such as burins;
IV – notches and denticulates. Handaxes were treated separately.

Typical Mousterian:	Characterized mainly by side-scrapers, with some denticulates and points. Handaxes and backed knives are rare or absent.
Ferrassie Mousterian:	Dominated by side-scrapers and rare in tools of group IV; handaxes are all but absent. Use of the Levallois technique is common.
Quina Mousterian:	Contains high numbers of side-scrapers, often with heavy scalar retouch (overlapping like the scales on fishskin). Low representation of notches and denticulates. The main distinction with the Ferrassie variant is in the poor Levallois component.
Denticulate Mousterian:	Dominant forms are those in group IV, with few tools of group III. Handaxes are likewise absent.
Mousterian of Acheulian Tradition (MAT):	So-called because of the presence of triangular or cordiform, flat-based handaxes, plus side-scrapers, denticulates and points. The MAT is sub-divided into two successive facies: **MAT A:** Handaxes are fairly common as are side-scrapers on by-products of handaxe manufacture. Backed knives are rare. Denticulates and examples of Upper Palaeolithic tools are more numerous than in other Mousterian facies. **MAT B:** Few handaxes and side-scrapers but relatively high proportions of backed knives and denticulates.

slotted into handles or shafts and easily replaced. Moreover, the cutting edge of individual artefacts was considerably lengthened by arranging them in a row. Blade making also increased the number of tool edges otherwise obtainable from a single block of flint and thus is a highly efficient use of raw material.

For the manufacture of longish blades the initial stages of preparing the core are crucially important and require patience (**11**). After preliminary shaping of the core with a stone hammer, long blades could then be detached successively with a heavy antler hammer or a soft stone equivalent. According to John Lord, the

curvature of the blades can be controlled by striking the edge of the core either obliquely or by using a more intrusive method. Of importance too is the type of hammer used and the degree of platform preparation. For example, in some Upper Palaeolithic industries (e.g. Magdalenian) the blades are quite curved, with carefully isolated

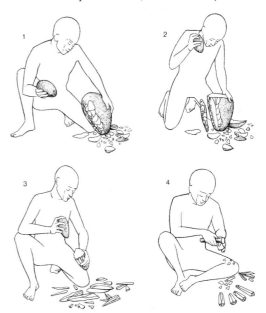

11 Successive stages in blade-making. 1 The core is prepared with a dense stone hammer. The front of the core is carefully crested (bifacially flaked to create a keel). 2 One, or sometimes two, platforms at opposite ends of the core are made before the crested blade is detached. This sets up parallel ridges which guide the direction of subsequent removals. 3 Blades are struck with a soft-stone or antler hammer. 4 The resulting blade blanks are converted into end-scrapers with a soft antler hammer.

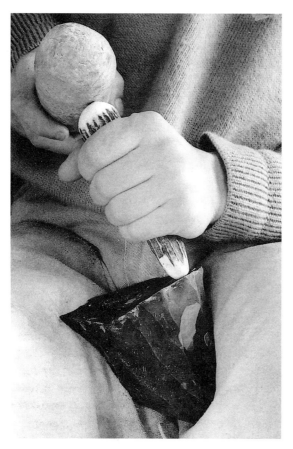

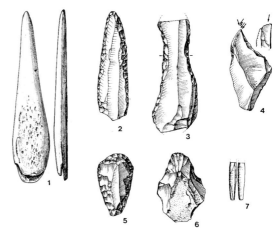

13 Mode 4 Upper Palaeolithic industry. Selected tools: 1 split-based point, 2 Aurignacian blade, 3 strangled blade, 4 busked burin, 5 scraper on retouched flake, 6 nosed/carinated scraper, 7 Dufour bladelet.

12 The 'punch' technique. Blades made by indirect percussion using a wooden billet and antler punch.

platforms and showing evidence of antler percussion. Others (e.g. Federmesser), on the other hand, have straight blades, with thicker platforms and less preparation, and were detached with a soft stone hammer (see **3** and **4**).

In the past there has been much discussion over whether or not indirect percussion was ever used in the Upper Palaeolithic. The indirect method is based on an intermediary 'punch' of antler which has the benefit of giving greater control and accuracy in delivering the percussive blow (**12**). Unfortunately, the characteristic traits of this method are indistinguishable from those left by direct percussion (antler hammer) making it difficult to demonstrate its use in the past. Ultimately, it may have been a question of skill and personal preference: but since fewer

breaks tend to happen with a punch, it might have been a useful tool for finishing wafer-thin artefacts, such as Solutrean leaf points (**colour plate 3**).

One of the defining characteristics of the Upper Palaeolithic is the range and diversity of tool-types made on blades. Following the typological classification of French prehistorians Denise Sonneville-Bordes and Jean Perrot, ninety-two different forms can be listed. They range from single tools such as end of blade scrapers and piercers to multiple tool types which had been converted at both ends. One common tool form is the burin which has chisel-like edges (**13**). It is believed to have been connected with making bone and antler equipment, one of the main technological innovations of the Upper Palaeolithic.

In this chapter we have briefly considered some of the main stone artefact categories which characterize the Palaeolithic and allow us to group them in a relative sequence. In the next chapter we shall turn our attention to the broader issues of chronology and climatic change which provide a necessary context for studying the past.

2
The Big Chill:
past environments and climate
changes in the Ice Age

What is an ice age?

To many people the idea of an 'Ice Age' no doubt conjures up shivery images of a polar landscape lashed by blizzards of freezing hail and snow, and inhabited only by a few, miserable looking, hairy-coated mammoths. But this view, however exaggerated, could hardly be less accurate. We now know, for example, that the 'Ice Age' description is actually rather misleading since it implies only a single 'big freeze' event, whereas in fact there were numerous successive episodes of ice advance and retreat during the period in question.

Responsibility for introducing the term can be traced back to the geologist Edward Forbes, who, writing in 1846, equated the Pleistocene (or 'most recent' geological period) with the 'Ice Age' or 'Glacial Epoch'. Among the most distinctive features of this period were cycles of intensive cold when glacial ice sheets expanded on a scale not seen in any earlier epoch. According to conservative estimates, the Pleistocene lasted 1.8 million years (based on palaeomagnetic evidence). It ended about 10,000 bp being replaced by the Holocene (meaning 'wholly new') epoch, which is the warm phase in which we live today.

Originally, only four major ice advances or glaciations were recognized in the Pleistocene. The evidence came from geological deposits in the Swiss Alps, described by the geographers Penck and Brückner in 1909. They were among the first geologists to demonstrate convincingly that the expansion and contraction of Alpine glaciers reflected long-term changes in the earth's climatic history.

Since then, many more cold and warm phases have been identified. For example, during the past 800,000 years or so there have been roughly nine major advances of ice which covered much of North America and Europe. The coldest phases of maximum ice advance are known as *glacials* (or cold stages) and these are separated by warmer episodes of climate referred to as *interglacials* (or warm stages). In addition to the main climatic events, other much shorter episodes of warming (*interstadials*) and cooling (*stadials*) can be detected within the main cold and warm stages. Generally speaking, during glacials, conditions in the mid-latitudes (i.e. Britain) were cold enough for arctic environments to develop, while in the warm interglacial phases the temperatures were occasionally higher than those of the present day. We can therefore assume that we are presently living in one of the longer warm intervals or interglacials which began between 14,000 and 13,000 years ago.

Thus, the period of the Pleistocene ice ages is one marked by climatic instability with periods of major cooling interspersed with warming phases of varying length and intensity. It is against this fluctuating climatic background that the human occupation of Britain and Europe has to be understood.

Records of past climate and environmental change

A diverse array of biological, chemical and geological indicators provide evidence of environments and climatic regimes in the Pleistocene. These sources are usually referred to as proxy records because they provide indirect, rather than absolute, evidence of conditions in the past. Among the most detailed sources of information on former climates and environments are those which can be inferred from deep-sea cores, ice cores and long terrestrial pollen sequences. Each of these methods allows climatic effects to be modelled and reconstructed though they do not always give entirely complementary results.

Deep-sea cores

One of the main sources for understanding the earth's past climate comes from deep-sea cores. The information is provided in mud deposits deep under the sea within which are found the skeletons of marine micro-organisms known as Foraminifera (or forams for short). Changes in the chemical composition of these creatures give us a more or less continuous record of changing global ice volume over time, as well as information on temperature changes in the world's oceans.

The way the method works is relatively simple: each tiny single-celled foram absorbs different oxygen isotopes during the course of its lifetime. The invisible isotopes (^{16}O and ^{18}O) are contained in sea water and are absorbed in their shells. When the creature dies it sinks to the sea floor and its shell is trapped in accumulating sediments. The proportion of one isotope to another (expressed as $\delta^{18}O$) is important because it varies according to global ice volume (14). The shells therefore contain a unique isotopic record of cold glacial/warm interglacial fluctuations in the earth's history.

Sediment cores of the ocean bed reveal changes in the isotopic composition of the different sediment beds. Over the past 800,000 years, the temperature curve based on the forams

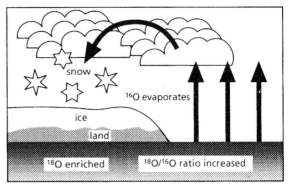

Glacial

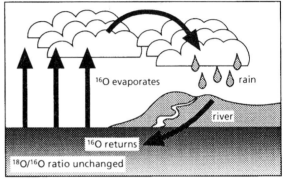

Interglacial

14 Principle of oxygen-isotope analysis. During cold stages (glacials) the oceans display a slight loss of the lighter isotope (^{16}O), which is evaporated and then precipitated in falling snow on the polar ice sheets. Conversely, during warm stages (interglacials), meltwaters containing greater volumes of ^{16}O are released back into the oceans, resulting in an unchanged $^{18}O/^{16}O$ ratio.

can be divided into nineteen or so oxygen-isotope stages (abbreviated as OIS) (15), each of which is numbered and represents a warm or cold stage. Numbering from the top down, the sequence documents successive stages. Odd numbers identify warm stages (we are currently living in OIS 1), while even numbers represent cold stages. Knowing how long each stage lasted is dependent on the existence of datable 'benchmarks' in the core sequences and the assumption that the accumulation of sediments occurred at a relatively constant rate. The fact that the results from different cores taken from various oceanic areas can be matched shows that the oxygen isotope record reflects global climatic events and not just local or regional ones.

Oxygen-isotope sequences are dated by two principle methods: radiocarbon (^{14}C) dating may be used to date sediments in the upper part of the cores, but once beyond the limits of the method (currently about 40,000–50,000 years), palaeomagnetism provides the best means of dating. Palaeomagnetic dating method is based on the principle that changes are constantly occurring in the earth's magnetic field (reflected in the direction of compass north). On some occasions in the past there have been wholesale magnetic reversals when the north pole and south pole have literally switched over. Such events and even smaller excursions away from the poles are fossilized in the form of remnant magnetism in sediments raised from the sea bed. The direction of compass north in these sediments can be matched with that occurring in datable volcanic deposits on the land and from this a reliable timescale can be reconstructed.

There have been four palaeomagnetic reversals since the beginning of the Pleistocene. The last major event of this kind occurred about 780,000 years ago, and is known as the Brunhes–Matuyama boundary. It is an important marker horizon useful for dating marine and terrestrial sequences alike. Based on the two dating methods (and assuming constant depositional rates) it can be shown that there have been something in the order of ten interglacials and ten glacials in this period. Current estimates suggest that the last nine interglacials each lasted between 10,000 and 20,000 years (**Table 2**).

Ice cores

A great deal of research has been devoted over the past fifteen years to the study of ice cores taken from thick ice sheets in Greenland and Antarctica. The cores provide a remarkable testimony of climatic change because they give a high-frequency picture of temperature shifts, based on *annual* records, extending back over long periods of time. The remarkable similarity

of the Arctic and Antarctic records implies a relatively uniform picture of climatic change on a worldwide scale. Currently, some of the longest sequences are known from the Greenland ice cores (**16**) which have drilled down through over 3,000m (10,000ft) of ice, and provide, in astonishing detail, a record of palaeoclimatic change extending back over 110,000 years. (The Antarctic cores now claim even longer records of up to 300,000 years.) In addition to isotopic content, the climatic signal is reconstructed from other chemical and physical analyses of the ice and tiny dust particles trapped within it. One of the most fascinating pieces of evidence to emerge from the ice cores is the extreme rapidity of many of the climatic oscillations.

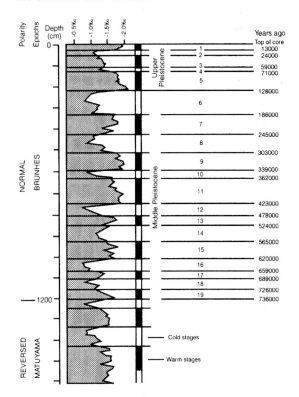

15 Deep-sea core sediment core V28-238 showing main isotope stages 1–19. Odd numbers represent warm stages (interglacials) and even numbers the cold stages (glacials). The Brunhes–Matuyama geomagnetic boundary is a worldwide event, now dated to about 780,000 years ago.

Table 2 *Sequence of marine cold and warm stages (OIS) and possible correlation with land-based records.*

Conventional British stages	Modified Scheme	Sites	Dutch/European sequence	OIS
	Flandrian		Holocene	1
Devensian	Devensian		Weichselian	5d+
Ipswichian	Ipswichian	Bobbitshole, Trafalgar Square	Eemian	5e
	Cold stage			6
	Temperate/ interglacial stage	Marsworth, Stanton Harcourt		7
Not classified	Cold stage		Saalian Complex	8
	Hoxnian	Hoxne?, Little Thurrock, Globe Pit, Purfleet		9
Wolstonian	Cold stage			10
Hoxnian	Temperate/ interglacial stage	Swanscombe, Barnham, Beeches Pit, Clacton	Holsteinian	11⁻
Anglian	Anglian		Elsterian	12
Cromerian	Temperate/ interglacial stage	Boxgrove, High Lodge, Wivenhoe, Westbury-sub-Mendip, Kent's Cavern, Warren Hill, Waverley Wood	Cromerian IV	13

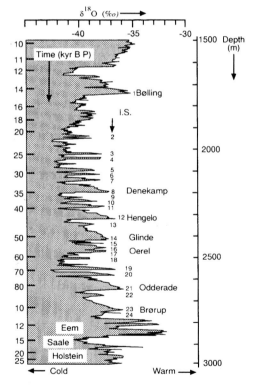

16 GRIP Greenland Summit Ice Core showing record of climatic change over the last 150,000 years. The sequence shows twenty-four separate interstadial events (IS/Ice Stage numbers) during the course of the last cold stage. Also indicated are the equivalent stages of the land-based pollen record.

The principle behind the method is again deceptively simple. Snow falling annually on Greenland glaciers gradually turns to ice. Trapped in the ice are tiny dust particles which accumulate as visible bands each summer as the surface of the glacier melts and refreezes. By counting the ice and dust bands it is possible to obtain an incremental record of ice growth from modern times back as far as the last interglacial and beyond. Dating can be cross-checked by ^{14}C measurements at the upper end of the sequence.

Interpreting the temperature signal of the ice record relies on isotopes precipitated in the form of snow and on chemical particles blown on to the Greenland ice caps. The latter include sodium and chloride from sea salt and ammonium from vegetation and can provide an estimate of past temperatures. Cool stadials are characterized by increases in dust and sea salt, while levels are depleted during warm interstadials. Estimates reveal that in the last glaciation (OIS 5d-2) there were at least twenty warm interstadials in the period 105,000–20,000 years ago, each 7°C warmer than the intervening cool stadials. Ice core data also confirm that many of the interstadials were short-lived, lasting in the region of between 500 and 2,000 years.

Among the most intriguing evidence to emerge recently has been that the change from cool to warm phases may have been extremely rapid, perhaps within the space of fifty years or less and thus well within a single human lifetime. However, it should be borne in mind that shifts from warm to cool climate generally occurred much more gradually in a series of step-like progressions. It is also clear that global temperatures are amplified in the polar regions and so may not reflect exactly the conditions experienced in lower latitudes.

The causes of these changes are not well understood (see below), but it is interesting that in both the ice cores and the deep-sea records these abrupt events are sometimes marked by enormous build-ups of dust. The source of this dust can be shown geologically to emanate from flotillas of icebergs which appear to expand, break up and discharge dust into the oceans and atmosphere (called Heinrich Events, see below). The latest such event matches the Younger Dryas Stadial which represents the final period of major ice regrowth in the British Isles. Claims have recently been made for similar phenomena in French lake sediments and even in windblown deposits in China.

Pollen cores

Climatic studies have for a long time relied on the analysis of fossil pollen grains trapped in land and lake sediments. The principle is well known; climatic oscillations produce changes in vegetation and these can be deduced from analogues found in the pollen spectra produced by modern plants and trees. Comparisons with fossil beetle data have shown that changes in vegetation composition take place relatively slowly and are therefore often unresponsive to short-term climatic oscillations. Nevertheless, pollen analysis remains an extremely useful tool for identifying shifting vegetation patterns that accompanied glacial–interglacial cycles. Long sequences of pollen change are preserved in deep lake sediments. These can be independently dated using ^{14}C, palaeomagnetism and, in some cases,

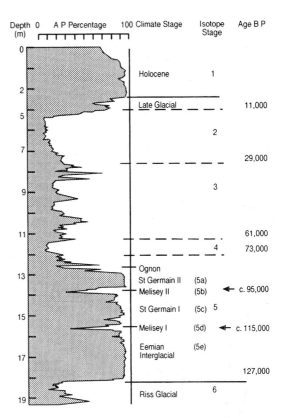

17 La Grande Pile pollen sequence of climatic change. The dates for the upper part of the sequence are based on radiocarbon measurements, while those lower down have been estimated on the basis of comparisons with the deep-sea core stages.

by dating associated volcanic ash beds. Some of the longest continuous pollen sequences in Europe come from the sites of La Grande Pile (**17**) in the Vosges and Les Echets near Lyon in eastern France. Complimentary records are also known from infilled lakes in the Eifel region in Germany, in southern Italy and the Massif Central, as well as two famous sites in Greece (Ioannina and Tenaghi Phillipon). Together, they provide a remarkable vegetational prehistory spanning the last 150,000 years and offer the possibility of correlating the land and sea records.

What drives ice ages?

Some of the processes affecting climatic change are now reasonably well understood: one of the most immediate appears to be ocean surface temperatures created by warm water Gulf Stream Drift currents which wash in from the Atlantic and keep Europe's climate fairly mild throughout the year. Without the warm insulating effects of these currents it is estimated (based on information for comparable latitudes in eastern Canada) that the climate of the British Isles would be on average 3°C cooler than it is at present.

The actual mechanism controlling these currents seems relatively straight-forward. It relies on a global system of deep water circulation referred to as the 'Ocean Conveyor' (18). The term vividly describes the idea of a moving belt of surface water which, in the North Atlantic, conducts warm ocean currents towards Britain, where they sink to form a returning deep-water mass of cooler (saltier) waters. It is

18 The Ocean Conveyor. A global system of oceanic circulation in which salt-laden deep water forms in the North Atlantic and eventually flows into the Pacific. Flow in the Atlantic may have been interrupted during cold episodes and was replaced by another mode of operation contributing to intense cooling and ice formation in the northern hemisphere.

known that if this continuous circulation were to be broken or disrupted it would have serious consequences for the climate of western Europe. Indeed, the potential effects could extend well beyond this region as illustrated by the El Niño phenomenon of today. This warm ocean current periodically wells up along the coast of Peru causing sea surface temperatures to rise, and has demonstrable effects in triggering droughts and floods, forest fires and major crop failures across diverse parts of the globe.

According to many experts, fluctuations in the conveyor have taken place at various times in the past (19). For example, today the 'door' in the North Atlantic is wide open, allowing warm subtropical waters to permeate north and keep our seas ice free. However, for much of the last glaciation the same 'door' appears to have been shut. Warm waters were unable to penetrate north, and this led to intense cooling of the North Atlantic, allowing ice sheets to grow. Even during a cold stage, however, the 'door' occasionally swung open for brief periods. The ice core record shows that one cause of such interruptions in the glacial climate is likely to have been periodic collapses in the

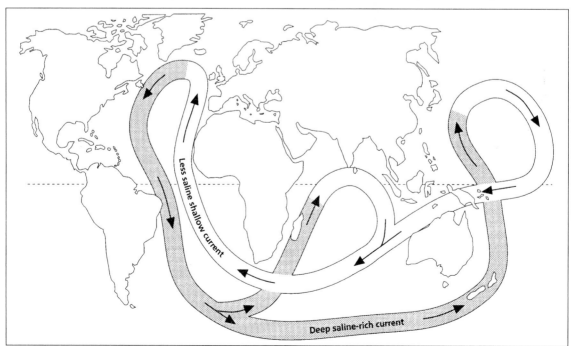

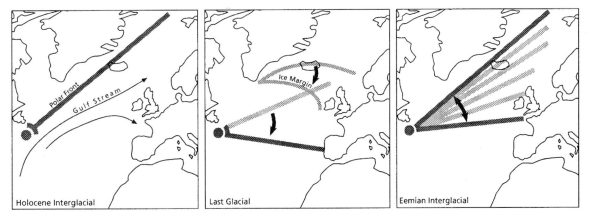

Holocene Interglacial   Last Glacial   Eemian Interglacial

North American ice sheet. These apparently led to enormous surges in iceberg formation, releasing rock dust particles on the ocean floor (the Heinrich Events mentioned earlier). Once iceberg activity had ceased and the ice margin had retreated further inland, the northwards movement of warm subtropical waters was again resumed. The overall effect was the creation of an unstable glacial climate, oscillating rapidly between cold stadial and warm interstadial conditions.

Past fluctuations in oceanic circulation patterns are not the only explanation for climatic change. Other contributory factors include past (and present) build-up of atmospheric greenhouse gases (carbon dioxide, methane, etc) and possibly volcanic activity, but neither of these is regarded as the prime underlying cause of ice ages. Instead, there is a general consensus that external forcing factors have much to do with driving ice ages.

To explain, we need to turn briefly to the subject of astronomy. For a long time it has been known that variations in the earth's orbit in relation to the sun, moon and other planets affect the intensity of radiation reaching the earth's surface. This led James Croll, and subsequently the geophysicist Milutin Milankovitch, to advance the 'Astronomical theory of ice ages'. They assumed that global surface temperatures would vary according to regular and predictable changes in the earth's orbit and axis. In other words, the amount of received solar radiation depends on three factors: the eccentricity of the

19 The effects of changing oceanic circulation patterns. The North Atlantic polar front (the circulation boundary between cold polar and warm water masses) may be viewed as a door which opens and shuts in the course of climatic shifts between interglacial and glacial conditions. The southernmost position of the door signals a cold climatic episode in the northern hemisphere. Today the Polar Front is in the northernmost position.

earth's orbit as it circles the sun; the tilt on its axis and its top-like wobble (or precession) as the earth spins on its axis (**20**). Each of these factors produces continuous effects. The main ones recognized by Milankovitch were a 100,000 year cycle (eccentricity of orbit), a 40,000 year cycle (tilt) and a 23,000 cycle (wobble). Today it is widely recognized that at least some of the dominant frequencies in the ocean and ice core records reflect similar cycles and therefore give greater plausibility to the model.

In addition to the longer cycles, shorter ones are also visible in the ice records. They occur over 11,100-year and 6,100-year periods and may be linked to the precession of the earth's axis. According to some authorities on the subject there have been twelve peaks in the 6,100-year cycle over the past 70,000 years and seven of them are associated with massive surges of icebergs in the North Atlantic (the so-called Heinrich Events). The Heinrich Events have, of course, been recognized in the ocean record and are linked to distinct cooling episodes.

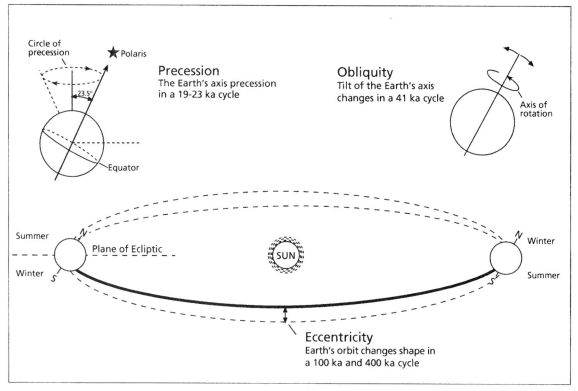

20 Orbital factors affecting the amount of solar radiation reaching the Earth's surface. Each of the cycles is expressed in ka (thousand years).

Before closing this section, it must be acknowledged that not everyone agrees with the Milankovitch theory. For example, other external forcing factors may also have played a prominent role in regulating global ice growth. One of the most recently discussed ideas is the effect of interplanetary dust particles entering the earth's atmosphere. According to new estimates measured from deep-sea cores, the levels of helium introduced by dust particles seem to correlate well with the 100,000-year periodicity already noted in solar radiation. The influx of minute dust particles may thus have caused subtle atmospheric changes which in turn affected rainfall and other weather patterns on a global scale.

The British record of climatic change

So far we have generalized about climatic change on a global scale. Now we will turn to consider briefly the British glacial record. As stated above, one of the greatest difficulties in undertaking such a task is how to match the land-based and oceanic/ice core records satisfactorily. According to the distribution of geological deposits in Britain (e.g. glacial tills and periglacial loess and coversands), there is evidence of only a limited number of major ice advances (**21**), far fewer than is indicated in the vastly more complicated sequence of cold–warm stages in the oceanic/ice core data. The potential for recognizing some of these has, of course, already been partially realized in the analysis of deep, continuous pollen cores like those from Grande Pile and Les Echets, mentioned above. But, this still leaves considerable problems in tackling more fragmentary terrestrial sequences and assembling them in correct chronological order over long timespans.

Now, using a range of dating techniques and with reference to biological and sediment history, a much more detailed land-based record of climatic change is beginning to emerge, although there are still a number of major gaps.

In addition to pollen, mollusc and beetle evidence, complementary sources of information come from the analysis of fossil bones found in caves and open-air sites. These include not only large animal species but also smaller rodents, birds, fish and reptiles. The small mammal faunas are particularly useful indicators because they (and their modern equivalents) are highly sensitive to climatic change and some have specialized dietary requirements. Thus, they provide valuable insight into local vegetational patterns and enable detailed palaeoclimatic reconstruction.

A further refinement has also been added which has led to much closer agreement between the number of warm stages present in the land-based record and that of the marine isotope stratigraphy. This is largely the work of the palaeontologist Andrew Currant and his students. The scheme is based on changes in the composition of faunal groupings found in stratified sediments which reflect successive

22 Selection of interglacial large mammals.
Top left, clockwise (not to scale): macaque, beaver, wild horse, wild pig, hippo, brown bear, Merck's rhino, narrow-nosed rhino, aurochs and roe deer.

warm (interglacial) stages. Specifically, he has been able to identify five different groups or assemblages of animal species indicative of past temperate woodland conditions (**Table 3**). These, he suggests, coincide with the warmer phases of interglacials (**22**). Currant's five groups share in common mammal species which are alive today (our present interglacial) and are indicative of closed deciduous woodland. The most typical indicator species are wood mice and bank voles as well as larger mammals such as roe deer and pigs (**23**).

As **Table 3** shows, therefore, the fossil-bone record is helping to fill the gaps in the British climatic record. By analyzing interglacial-type faunas it is now possible to order them in a general sequence and to recognize more warm stages in the land sediments than was

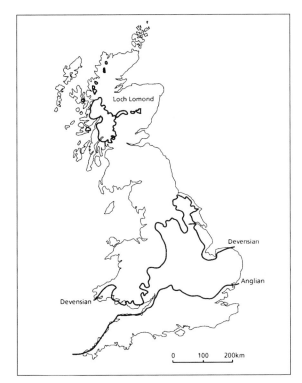

21 Map of Britain showing maximum ice advances for the Anglian and Devensian cold stages.

Table 3
Key fossil mammal assemblages associated with woodland interglacial conditions
in the British Pleistocene sequence. Currant's groups are ranked from 1 to 5 (youngest to oldest).
The sixth group (0) represents native mammals of the present Holocene epoch.

Fauna	Group					
	0	1	2	3	4	5
Wood mouse (*Apodemus sylvaticus*)	*	*	*	*	*	*
Bank vole (*Clethrionomys glareolus*)	*	*	*	*	*	*
Roe deer (*Dama dama*)	*	*	*	*	*	*
Wild pig (*Sus scrofa*)	*	*	*	*	*	*
Extinct water vole (*Mimomys savini*)						*
Extinct water vole (*Arvicola cantiana*)		*	*	*	*	
Extinct rhino (*Stephanorhinus hundsheimensis*)					*	*
Extinct giant beaver (*Trogontherium cuvieri*)				*	*	*
Extinct cave bear (*Ursus spp*)				*	*	*
Macaque (*Macaca sylvanus*)			*	*		*
Beaver (*Castor fiber*)	*		*	*	*	*
Wild horse (*Equus ferus*)			*	*	*	*
Humans (*Homo*)	*		*	*	*	
Merck's rhino (*Stephanorhinus kirchbergensis*)			*	*		
Narrow-nosed rhino (*Stephanorhinus hemitoechus*)		*	*	*		
Aurochs (*Bos primigenius*)	*	*	*	*		
White-toothed shrew (*Crocidura spp*)			*			
Brown bear (*Ursus arctos*)	*	*	*			
Hippo (*Hippopotamus amphibius*)		*				

Group 5:
Apart from woodland indicators, this warm temperate faunal assemblage includes an important chronological marker in the extinct water vole (*Mimomys*). The vole has rooted molars as distinct from its evolutionary descendant which has continuously growing (i.e. rootless) teeth. This evolutionary grade is known to be commonest in the Middle Pleistocene before about 500,000 years ago. Group 5 faunal assemblages occur in deposits at West Runton, Norfolk, where they are dated to the earlier part of the Cromerian Interglacial Complex, possibly correlating with OIS 15.

Group 4:
The small vertebrates now include the evolved grade of vole (*Arvicola*) with increased crown height and rootless molars. Although the animals present are of broadly similar composition to those in Group 5, pig is notably absent. This faunal group is identified in the 'Pink Breccia' unit at Westbury-sub-Mendip, Somerset and in Unit 4c in the Slindon Silts at Boxgrove, West Sussex. Boxgrove is also an early site from which human remains have been recorded in the British Isles. It is at present correlated with OIS 13.

Group 3:
A feature of this group is a decrease in diversity in small mammals. In the megafauna two species of rhinoceros are now present and aurochs makes its first appearance in the British Pleistocene. Deposits containing this fauna are found at Swanscombe, Kent, and at Clacton, Essex, and are associated with the Hoxnian interglacial. Despite considerable disagreement about the age of this warm temperate stage, it may correlate with OIS 11.

Group 2:
Distinguishable from previous groups by the occurrence of one or more species of white-toothed shrew. The megafauna now includes brown bear instead of more archaic spelaeoid forms, but otherwise is consistent with the earlier groups in sharing temperate woodland species such as macaque. Faunas of this kind have been recognized at Gray's Thurrock and Cudmore Grove, Essex as well at Tornewton Cave, Devon. They may belong to OIS 9 or OIS 7. Based on more recent research work by Danielle Schreve, there is now some suggestion that faunas in this group can be split into two distinctive sub-groups corresponding to the separate OIS warm stages.

Group 1:
This group comprises the famous *Hippopotamus* fauna found in Britain as far afield as Trafalgar Square, Central London, and Victoria Cave, North Yorkshire. Only one species of rhino is present; notable absentees amongst the other mammals are horse, macaque and beaver. The hippo fauna is widely believed to coincide with a period of highest global sea level in OIS 5e. Interestingly, this is a period for which there is currently no fossil or artefactual evidence of human activities in the British Isles.

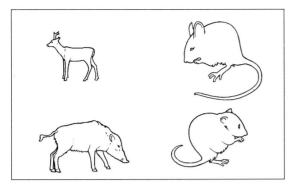

23 Interglacial temperate woodland indicators for Britain. Top left, clockwise (not to scale): roe deer, wood mouse, bank vole and wild pig.

imaginable even ten years ago. This has important implications for understanding environmental changes through time and provides a context for discussing the human occupation of Britain in the Palaeolithic.

A brief synopsis of climatic changes in Britain and Europe over the last 150,000 years

According to some sources, accurate correlations between the oceanic/ice core and pollen records are now possible over a continuous period extending from 150,000 years ago to the present. This provides the background for examining Neanderthal and modern human activities in Britain (discussed in Chapters 5–8).

c. 150,000–127,000 years ago (Oxygen Isotope Stage – OIS 6) Glacial

A cold stage in which ice sheets extended over much of northern Britain, leaving the south covered by a vegetational mosaic of cold tundra and open steppe. Regions north of 45° had permanently frozen ground. Pollen evidence from France indicates that the climate was colder and drier with mean annual temperatures depressed to 1–2°C (as compared to c. 9–10°C at present). Sea-levels had dropped more than 100m below today's limit. A major land-bridge still connected Britain with Europe. British fauna recorded from this period are dominated

by cold species such as mammoth, woolly rhino, reindeer, and arctic fox.

127,000–117,000 years ago (OIS 5e) Interglacial (**24**)

Ice core data reveal an abrupt climatic transition between OIS 6 and OIS 5e. Mean annual temperatures rose by as much as 10°C, reaching a summer maximum of 16–18°C. The climate was thus considerably warmer than it is today, with hot summers and mild winters. Plants such as water chestnut grew in Britain. The land-bridge was submerged by very high sea-levels (5–6m/16–20ft higher than today), which drowned large areas of the Low Countries and parts of south-east Britain. French pollen evidence displays a typical interglacial succession of forest development commencing with birch and pine, followed by broad-leafed

24 Reconstructed vegetational patterns for the last interglacial (OIS 5e). Warmer than average conditions led to high sea levels, submerging parts of the Low Countries, northern Germany and southern Scandinavia (stippled areas). During this period Britain was an island and there is no evidence of human occupation.

deciduous woodland (oak, elm, hazel and yew) and then a reversion to more coniferous species (fir, spruce and pine). A surprising absentee in the tree flora was beech, which may be explained by widespread competition from the hornbeam. Among the animals documented in Britain in this period were species such as hippopotamus and the European pond tortoise. Humans do not appear to have been present in the British Isles.

117,000–75,000 years ago (OIS 5a–5d) cool temperate

A gradual deterioration in climate characterized by a series of warm interstadial (5c and 5a) and cool stadial (5d and 5b) oscillations. The cool phases were cold enough for European ice sheets to re-expand and the vegetation in cool stadials 5d and 5b of grasses, sedges and other tundra-like plants reflects markedly open periglacial conditions. However, the rapidity of tree expansion in interstadials 5c and 5a suggests that the stadials were not cold enough to limit tree growth altogether. Interstadial deposits recorded at Chelford and Wretton in southern Britain most probably correlate with 5c. Sea-levels fell to a low of about 50m (160ft) below present mean sea-level near the end of 5d but rose again slightly after that. In northern Europe the interstadials were sufficiently warm for birch and coniferous forest to become established but temperatures never again attained those of 5e. The impact of these oscillations, with their steep climatic gradients, must have had significant effects on faunal populations. There is no certain evidence of human occupation in Britain even during the interstadials.

75,000–60,000 years ago (OIS 4) very cold

The onset of intensely cold conditions in Europe was marked by advances in the Scandinavian ice sheet, although most of Britain, south of the latitude of the Isle of Man, probably remained ice free. Pollen evidence from France shows a brief phase of coniferous forest but otherwise this period in northern Europe seems to have been

characterized entirely by open tundra vegetation. Mean annual temperatures dropped on average to 12–13°C below present, dipping to an arctic −20 to −25°C in the coldest winter months. The dry North Sea plain made our climate much more continental with short, mild summers and long, cold winters. Native faunas were dominated by bison and reindeer with a mixture of carnivores including wolf, leopard, wolverine (glutton) and a very large species of brown bear. No artefacts or other signs of human activity have yet been recorded in association with this British *Banwell*-type fauna (see **26**).

60,000–25,000 years ago (OIS 3) cold dry (**25**)

This stage is typified by a sharply oscillating climate which shows up clearly in the Greenland ice cores. Short cooling episodes (lasting up to

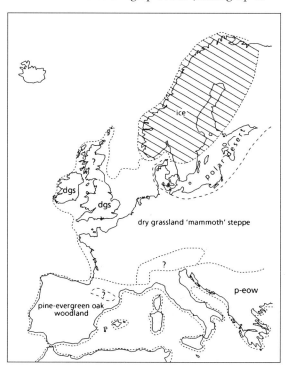

25 Reconstructed vegetational patterns for the early last glacial (OIS 3). Cold, dry conditions left large areas of Europe, including Britain, dominated by rich grasslands. These were ideal habitats for a variety of steppe animals including mammoth, woolly rhino and horse. Human and animal populations probably crossed the land-bridge into Britain at the end of this period.

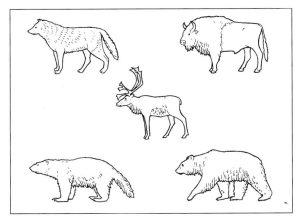

26 *Banwell*-type fauna. Includes animals such as (top left, clockwise) wolf, bison, reindeer, brown bear and wolverine (not to scale).

1,000 years) are terminated by Heinrich Events (see above) and a number of milder climatic episodes are recorded in the intervening periods. Reductions in global ice volumes resulted in sea levels ranging between 50m and 80m (160ft and 260ft) below present. During the mild intervals arboreal pollen indicates woodland development, but on a reduced scale compared to earlier interstadials (in OIS 5a and 5c). Birch and pine woodland grew in parts of eastern France and mean annual temperatures were perhaps 4°C below those of the present. Further west in Britain, the cool dry conditions encouraged development of rich arid grasslands (mammoth-steppe) which supported animals such as mammoth, woolly rhino, lion, bear, giant deer, horse and spotted hyena (**colour plate 4**) and wolf. The migration of these animals (**27**) into Britain probably also coincided with the arrival of Late Neanderthals. Their Mousterian culture is found in association with this so-called *Coygan*-type fauna. Towards the end of OIS 3, from about 31,000 bp, anatomically modern humans, with a distinctive Upper Palaeolithic culture, begin to appear in the British archaeological record.

25,000–13,000 years ago (OIS 2) full glacial Climatic conditions grew increasingly colder. The height of the glacial, corresponding to the maximum global ice volume as recorded in deep ocean cores, occurred at around 18,000 years ago The Greenland ice cores show temperatures as depressed as those in OIS 4. During its height, the Scandinavian ice sheet covered much of northern Europe and extended in Britain as far south nearly as Cardiff in south Wales (see **21**). Ice sheets estimated at over a mile thick (1,800m) existed in Scotland. Many periglacial deposits and landforms in Britain date to this period. An almost barren polar desert is reflected by a drop in mean annual temperatures to around 16–17°C lower than those of the present day. Plant growth was limited to various mosses, grasses and sedges. Under these conditions few large vertebrates are likely to have been present, except episodically or on a seasonal basis. Modern human populations seem to

27 *Coygan*-type fauna. Includes animals such as (top left, clockwise) cave lion, wild horse, spotted hyena, wolf, reindeer, mammoth, woolly rhino, brown bear (not to scale).

have retreated south of the Loire Valley in France for much of this period.

13,000 years ago to the present (OIS 1) Interglacial

The beginning of this period is marked by rapid warming (interstadial). Summer temperatures rose abruptly from 13,000 bp to a maximum of 17°C, but winter conditions remained cold (1°C) and dry. In Britain woodland dominated by tree birch expanded after about 12,000 bp against a background of declining temperatures. Faunal species known to have been present in the interstadial include mammoth, wild horse, red deer, wild cattle, brown bear, arctic hare, as well as infrequent visitors such as saiga antelope. After 11,000 bp conditions became very much cooler (stadial) and the global ice volume again increased. British beetle assemblages and pollen profiles indicate open tundra-like conditions, also reflected in the dominance of reindeer among the preserved large fauna. The end of the stadial is signalled by an episode of very rapid warming across Britain and western Europe, which some estimates suggest took less than fifty years! The ensuing period of climatic stability, which has so far lasted 10,000 years (Holocene), is markedly different from the earlier periods of the Pleistocene and offers an interesting contrast in terms of climatic modelling.

3
The earliest peopling of Europe

African genesis

Ever since Charles Darwin's bold prediction that the deepest roots of our ancestry would be found in Africa, scientific opinion has favoured that continent as the place where the human lineage was born. Nowadays there is an impressive body of evidence to support this view. For not only do the earliest dated fossil hominid finds occur in Africa, but nowhere else in the world have comparable examples been found before about 1.8 million years ago. Further signs of an original African ancestry are revealed by our strikingly close genetic links with higher primates, such as chimpanzees, who evolved in Africa and share more than 98 per cent of their molecular make-up with modern human beings.

Given the overwhelming evidence that our earliest human ancestors originated in Africa, it follows that at some point in the past, Europe and the rest of the world must have been colonized by populations moving out of Africa. In this chapter, we shall explore when and how Europe and Britain came to be inhabited, and by whom, and what conditions either forced, or enabled, hominids to move out of the tropics into the higher latitudes.

When did hominids extend their range beyond Africa?

When people first left the African continent and where in Eurasia they went are still highly controversial questions. Until recently, it had

been widely assumed that the earliest intercontinental dispersal of hominids occurred a little before 1.25 million years ago, as indicated by dated fossil finds of *Homo erectus* in China and Java (Indonesia). Now, however, this view has been thrown into considerable doubt by redating of ancient fossil beds in Java and fresh discoveries in Spain, Georgia and China which all suggest a much earlier migration out of Africa, perhaps around 1.8 million years ago or even earlier.

The new findings have caused another dilemma for palaeoanthropologists: which species of *Homo* was the first to extend its range beyond the confines of tropical Africa? Because of the new dating this prerogative must now go to a hominid living in Africa at least 1.8–1.9 million years ago. The difficulty is that around this time there are up to three candidates to choose from: *Homo rudolfensis*, until recently a leading contender for the first *Homo*; the more modern-looking *Homo ergaster* (the African ancestor of *Homo erectus*); and *Homo habilis*. To this collection can now be added a new fossil jaw of *Homo* from the Hadar region of Ethiopia which dates to 2.33 million years ago, though it is not yet clear whether it merits a species classification of its own (28).

Despite the current lack of clarity in the fossil record, at least one thing seems certain: after about 1.9 million years ago there is good evidence of a species recognizably like ourselves known as *Homo ergaster*. The most complete

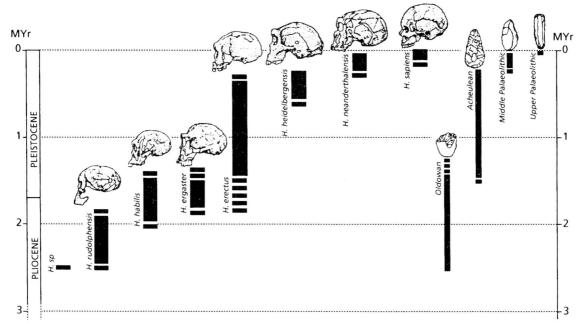

28 Time chart of the chronological range of the various species of the genus *Homo* and Palaeolithic cultural stages.

example of this kind is the so-called 'Turkana Boy', a 1.6-million-year old skeleton from Nariokotome, West Turkana in Kenya, discovered in 1984. The fossil of the 9–12-year-old child represents a big brained individual (roughly double the size of his forerunners) who, if he had lived to maturity, would have been 1.8m (6ft) tall. The brain size and build of this *Homo ergaster* species is considerably larger than any other of the early African hominids (*H. rudolfensis* and *H. habilis*), and bears the closest resemblance to the first fossils found outside Africa.

A further challenge posed by an earlier dispersal date concerns the technological capabilities of the first hominids to exit Africa. Traditionally, the initial African stone tool technologies have been divided into two kinds. The earliest, found in northern Kenya and Ethiopia and dating to about 2.5 million years ago, consists of rudimentary flakes, flake scrapers and simple 'core-like' pebble tools (known as a mode 1 industry) (see 7). There are

in fact sub-divisions of this oldest technology: the Ethiopian 'Omo-type' toolkits are considered to be slightly older and less technically accomplished than the 'Karari' and 'Oldowan' toolkits from elsewhere in East Africa. The second, slightly later technology is typified by teardrop-shaped tools, called handaxes (see 8), as well as a variety of small flake tools. In Africa this mode 2 industry (also described as Acheulian) is variously dated to 1.6 or 1.4 million years ago. Though Acheulian handaxe industries clearly represent a subsequent technological development (identified by progressive stages at sites like Olduvai Gorge, Tanzania), both mode 1 and mode 2 traditions continue to develop in parallel in Africa for some considerable time.

One of the main implications raised by redating the African dispersal is whether the very earliest populations to leave the tropics did so assisted only by simple mode 1 pebble tools or by Acheulian handaxes. Conventionally, the earliest dated Acheulian industry outside Africa comes from Ubeidiya in Israel (1.4 million years ago), but this is practically identical to the earliest Acheulian dates in East Africa from Orlorgesailie and Peninj (though evidence from

Konso-Gardula, Ethiopia is slightly earlier). For other parts of the Old World outside Africa, particularly in south and east Asia, handaxes of this very early stage are virtually non-existent and the lithic industries instead contain pebble tools. In the past this absence has been explained in terms of cultural 'memory loss' but if the new dating is correct then it would clearly support the idea that the first hominid wave to leave Africa did so before the Acheulian stage developed. The issue is brought more sharply into focus by the fact that the *Homo erectus* jaw from Dmanisi in Georgia, which may be as early as 1.8 million years old (but see below), was associated with a mode 1 industry of pebble tools and flakes. Based on this evidence and on potentially even earlier dates from China and Java (**Table 4**), it now seems clear that the initial appearance of *Homo* in the higher latitudes is linked to a pre-handaxe technology.

Natural obstacles facing the African emigrants

Before going on to discuss the possible causes of population dispersal, it is worth considering the potential natural obstacles confronting

hominids moving into the higher latitudes. To begin with, it should be recalled that early African hominids were first and foremost tropical creatures. In moving northwards into European temperate environments, they would have needed to adapt to markedly different conditions, not least the greater variations in seasonal temperature and the marked changes in daylight lengths between winter and summer. Since both of these factors effectively control the growth cycles of plants and animals this must have had enormous consequences for incoming populations. Indeed, it has recently been suggested that reduced winter levels of sunlight and plant growth, particularly in northern Europe, were the principal factors inhibiting the establishment of very early human populations in these areas.

In addition to these constraints, other natural obstacles would have included climatic barriers such as the extended areas of permafrost and the more southerly flow of colder air circulation especially during the glacial periods. At the same time, the existence of belts of temperate forest and grassland-steppe, as well as of cold deserts north of the 30–40° parallel, may each have acted as

Table 4

Dating of earliest hominid fossils and stone artefacts outside Africa.

Provenance	Age in millions of years ago	Hominid fossils	Lithic technology
Erq-el-Ahmar, Israel	1.96–1.78		flake-pebble
Ubeidiya, Israel (Upper Formation)	1.4		handaxe
Ubeidiya, Israel (Lower formation)	1.4		flake-pebble
Dmanisi, Georgia	1.4–1.8	*H. erectus*	flake-pebble
Riwat, Pakistan	1.96–1.78		flake-pebble
Longgupo, China	1.96–1.78	*Homo ?*	flake-pebble
Sangiran, Java	1.66	*H. erectus*	
Mojokerto, Java	1.81	*H. erectus*	
Ceprano, Italy	>0.78 ?	*H. erectus*	
Atapuerca, Spain (Gran Dolina TD6)	>0.78	*Homo sp*	flake-pebble
Fuente Neuva 3, Orce, Spain	0.99–<1.6		flakes
Venta Micena, Orce, Spain	1.8	*Homo ?*	
Barranco Leon, Orce, Spain	1.8		flakes

significant deterrents to migrating groups lacking appropriate technology.

Perhaps the most formidable of all natural checks to movement between Africa and Europe were the twin geographical barriers of the sea and mountains. Among the potential entry points into western Europe were routes into Iberia from North Africa via the Strait of Gibraltar and slightly further eastwards across into Sicily and Italy (**29**). In the absence of extensive land-bridges (at least over the past 2 million years) both of these routes entailed significant sea crossings. Of the two, the narrowest transit point

29 Map of potential routes into Europe and fossil localities for early *Homo*. Although very early dates have been recorded in Spain, an eastern route is currently most favoured. Also indicated is the 10°C isothermic line of the coldest month of the year, a suggested limiting factor in colonization. Site names: 1 Turkana, 2 Hadar, 3-4 Ubeidiya, Erq-el-Ahmar, 5 Dmanisi, 6 Ceprano, 7 Orce, 8 Atapuerca, 9 Riwat, 10 Longgupo, 11 Sangiran, 12 Mojokerto.

would have been between Ceuta and Gibraltar where a reduced gap of as little as 12km (7 miles), perhaps with some islands in between, may have existed during the ice age maxima. Despite the available options there are currently good reasons, explored later in the chapter, for believing that early hominids preferred another point of entry at the eastern end of the Mediterranean. The two most likely eastern routes into Europe are from Turkey into the Balkans via the Bosphorous Straits or a less direct overland route around the northern perimeter of the Black Sea. In both cases high mountain ranges would have blocked some of the journey, although it would have been theoretically possible to follow the coastal plain of western Turkey during periods of lower sea-level.

What conditions were necessary for hominids to leave Africa?

How then, with all of these apparent impediments to free movement, did ancestral human populations manage to disperse into

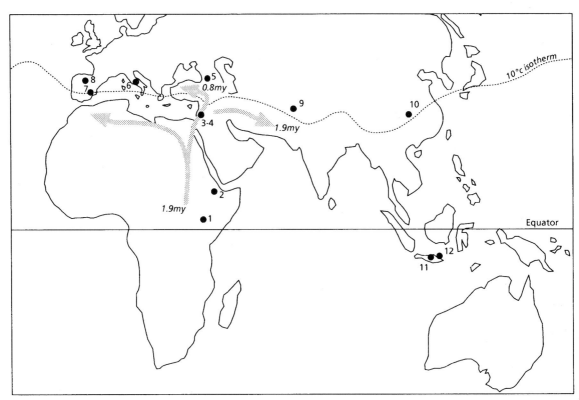

Europe? To answer this point we need to consider the question from two angles: what factors enabled hominids already adapted to warm tropical environments to migrate into cooler temperate environments, and what, if anything, triggered the migration episodes?

Anthropologist Rob Foley has proposed that one reason early hominids were able to extend beyond their tropical environments was that they had become much more successful at obtaining meat than their predecessors. He has pointed out that herbivores, such as antelopes, tend to be restricted to the plant resources in their local habitat, whereas the opposite is true of meat-eating carnivores. They are free to roam wherever meat is available and this means practically anywhere in the world. According to this view, once meat became an important component of the diet, *Homo* was no longer tethered to the African savanna, but was able to range as widely as other carnivores.

Some support for this idea is given by palaeontologist Alan Turner, who has shown that the extinction of various large carnivores in Africa may have left the way open for hominids to exploit the vacated food niches. According to him, earlier hominids would have competed for meat with scavenging carnivores, such as the hyena, but some 1.5 million years ago a number of hunting carnivores, like *Megantereon* – a leopard-sized cat – and a sabre-tooth cat, died out. It was precisely at this juncture, according to Turner, that *Homo erectus* (or *H. ergaster*) was able to take full advantage of this gap in the carnivore hierarchy and switched from a mainly scavenging to a hunting existence. Seen in this broader context, it may be relevant that ancestral humans were just one of a larger group of mammals that successfully expanded their ranges and occupied vast areas including Europe. Other early African carnivores such as the lion, leopard and wolf are thought to have arrived in Eurasia within the last 2 million years. It is interesting also to note that among the fauna recovered at Dmanisi in Georgia was a rather more unlikely immigrant from Africa – the ostrich!

Further evidence of the practical capabilities of these early hominids is the fact that they were able to harness the use of fire, as indicated by heavily burnt animal bones at Swartkrans in South Africa. The bones, dating to around 1 million years ago, were found in the upper layers of the cave with fossils of *Homo*. They showed the same degree of burning as would be expected in a campfire. The evidence suggests that by this time early *Homo* was increasingly able to manipulate the environment. Harnessing the power of fire provided sources of heat and light as well as protection against predators. It may also have allowed supplemental dietary options because heating can be used to break down poisonous toxins in plants and seeds, while roasting of meat kills harmful parasites. In the higher latitudes of Europe the ability to control fire would have conferred obvious advantages, enabling extra heat and light during the long winter months, and the ability to thaw frozen animal carcasses for food.

While certain pre-adaptations may have favoured *Homo ergaster* as the first hominid to leave Africa, what is much less clear are the underlying causes behind human and animal migrations. One option still preferred by many is that the main impetus behind the migrations was global climatic change. According to this view fluctuations between glacial periods and the warmer interglacials produced major changes in the geographical distribution of African savanna and rainforest belts. Higher rainfall (during interglacials) made some regions like the Sahara much easier to live in; while drier, cooler episodes (during glacials) would have driven human populations out. If, in some cases, the retreat southwards had been blocked then perhaps populations were propelled towards the Mediterranean coast and the Near East. Such an explanation, which sees the Sahara as a type of geographical 'pump', could account for the northwards expansion of people out of Africa. However, very little is known of the environmental conditions in the Sahara during the critical period around 1–2 million years ago.

Foley, however, expounds a different view of these events. He suggests that the prime moving force was an increased growth in regional populations. He believes this led to pressure on local resources and that hominids living in such situations were faced with a stark choice of either intensifying their use of an area or simply finding somewhere else to live. In Foley's view, the progressive spread of people could have been gradual, not so much a migration as a slow drifting of population caused by family groups regularly splitting and forming new territories nearby. Measured in individual human lifespans such movements must have seemed incredibly slow. But, even allowing for a relatively modest rate of 16 kilometres (10 miles) per decade, hominid populations could have covered 3,000 kilometres (1,875 miles), or roughly the distance between Kenya's Lake Turkana and Alexandria on the north African Mediterranean coast, in just under 1,900 years. In geological time, of course, such a migration would seem instantaneous.

First colonization of Europe

Although there is now a growing consensus that archaic hominids may have left Africa up to 1.8 million years ago (as demonstrated by the new discoveries from Georgia and the Far East), there is much less agreement over when Europe itself was first colonized. Archaeologists are generally divided along the following lines: those in favour of the 'long chronology', who believe that hominids entered Europe at least 1 million years ago, and those who prefer a more conservative estimate of roughly 500,000 years ago – the 'shorter chronology' school.

Adherents of the 'long chronology' are convinced that population movements into Europe could be potentially as old as any of the cited dating evidence for any of the other fossil sites outside Africa (**Table 4**). Such a view has been reinforced by new discoveries in Spain: at Atapuerca near Burgos, and further south at Orce in the province of Andalusia (**30**). Both sites have produced hominid remains, although

the identity of the Orce bones from the Venta Micena locality is still regarded as highly controversial. At Atapuerca Gran Dolina, significant hominid remains and stone artefacts of mode 1 type occur in horizon TD6, well below a level corresponding to the Brunhes–Matuyama palaeomagnetic boundary (see **15**). If correctly interpreted this would give the archaeological horizon an age in excess of 780,000 years. According to preliminary site reports, the finds are distinctive enough to assign them to a new species, *Homo antecessor* (from the Latin word meaning 'explorer'). But the idea is still rather controversial because the classification rests on an immature individual; the remains of an adult will be needed before the matter can be fully resolved. At Venta Micena, Orce (**15**), the dating evidence appears to be even earlier. Here, a layer containing putative hominid bones (a temporal fragment and the end of an arm bone) is situated slightly above a level with a claimed palaeomagnetic age of 1.8 million years, although other estimates are more conservative (**Table 4**). If the earlier estimate is taken at face value, it would suggest that movement of peoples into Europe took place more or less contemporaneously with the colonization of the Near East and Asia.

Opponents of the 'long chronology' strongly challenge the dating of the Orce sites, arguing instead for a much later appearance of hominids in Europe. They are fairly adamant that populations did not reach Europe, or at least northern Europe, until about 500,000 years ago. According to a strict set of criteria that they have set out (**Table 5**) none of the early evidence for occupation stands up to proper scrutiny. They dismiss the Orce claims on the grounds of the palaeomagnetic dating evidence and uncertainty over the identification of the Venta Micena hominid remains. They even call into question some of the very oldest Eurasian dates such as Dmanisi because of problems over dating. For example, at the Dmanisi site, the original date of 1.8 million years was obtained on a basalt flow from beneath the archaeological deposits. But,

Table 5

Criteria adopted by the 'short chronology' school against a very early colonization of Europe.

Sites before 500,000 years ago	Sites after 500,000 years ago
Characterized by:	Characterized by:
1 Small series of isolated pieces ('pseudoartefacts') selected from a natural pebble background	1 Large collections of excavated knapping floors with refitting material
2. 'Artefacts' found in a disturbed context	2 Primary context sites
3 Contested 'primitive' assemblages	3 Uncontested Acheulian and non-Acheulian industries
4 No human remains or doubtful fossils	4 Human remains common

following redating of the hominid layer it appears that the sediments were now laid down during a period of reversed polarity, and could be only 800,000 years old or even less. This view is also shared by palaeoanthropologists like Braüer who recognize in the jaw features a very late form of *Homo erectus*.

The arguments on this subject look set to continue for some time to come. In a further new twist to the debate in 1996, leading proponents of the 'shorter chronology' have shifted their ground slightly to accommodate the latest findings from Atapuerca Gran Dolina. According to the new stance they now accept that parts of the Mediterranean zone of Europe may have been occupied as early as 800,000 years ago.

This still leaves unresolved the question of the route by which early hominids first entered Europe. Some archaeologists still favour an easterly route with people arriving in southern Europe across the Bosphorus via Turkey (see **29**). From here they were free to gain access to the northern coastline of the Mediterranean, which might explain the relatively early dates for occupation in Spain. It may also be no coincidence that a late *Homo erectus* fossil with an estimated age of 700,000 years was recently discovered in Ceprano, Italy. One other reason for an eastern access point being preferred is because of the Ubeidiya site in Israel where *in situ* finds of handaxes have been dated to 1.4 million years ago. The alternative is that people entered Europe across the Strait of Gibraltar,

but this view is currently out of favour because none of the sites on the North African side is demonstrably older than about 800,000 years. Nevertheless, the issues are finely balanced and, if the Spanish investigators at Atapuerca are correct in their analysis, then it is even possible that more than one hominid lineage was involved in the early colonization of Europe.

If we accept the revised version of the 'shorter chronology' model, it still leaves unresolved the thorny issue of why people took so long to colonize northwards into Europe especially since they had arrived so early in the Near East. Despite the shortage of clearcut answers at present, one plausible explanation for the delay is that the first emigrants to leave Africa were still not capable of coping with the fully temperate environments of Europe beyond the Alps and Pyrenees. In other words, they were only able to expand into the Mediterranean ecological zones because they were broadly comparable to those of North Africa and the Near East. Some authors have even proposed that an invisible temperature barrier such as the 10°C isotherm (see **29**) acted to regulate the northwards expansion of hominids until around 500,000 years ago. An alternative explanation is that an earlier human colonization of Europe was prevented by competition from other carnivores, but this theory seems less likely given the relatively early evidence from Dmanisi.

In considering these various theories, it should not be underestimated how important a role the destructive forces of nature had to play in creating and preserving the archaeological record. It could be argued, for example, that the apparent delay in colonization of Europe north of the Pyrenees and the Alps was due more to the poor preservation of human evidence through landscape erosion than to any lack of human presence. This is because, unlike Africa, the Near East and parts of southern Europe, much of Britain and northern Europe have been covered by glaciers (see Chapter 2). Glacial processes have doubtless done much to wipe away former traces of activity, turning an extremely patchy record of human occupation into an even sparser and intermittent one. In the following chapter we shall examine in detail one of the rare exceptions of an early site in Britain which did manage to survive the destructive effects of successive glaciations.

The earliest British evidence for human activity

In the context of the debate concerning the earliest colonization of Europe, it is worth stressing that Britain has always been geographically isolated. Curiously this has less to do with it being an island, since for much of the past 1.8 million years there has been a dry land-bridge connection with the European mainland via the Dover Straits. Instead, a more influential factor seems to have been Britain's peripheral position on the extreme north-west margin of the continent. As a logical consequence populations arriving from the south inevitably took longer to filter into the marginal areas of Europe. Despite these observations, however, it is surprising to find that among the most accurately dated and oldest Palaeolithic sites in northern Europe are those from Britain (30).

Some of the earliest evidence for human occupation in Europe north of the Alps comes from the cave sites of Westbury-sub-Mendip (Somerset), Kent's Cavern (Devon), and the open-air locations of High Lodge (Suffolk) and Boxgrove (Sussex). At each of these sites artefacts have been recovered in deposits of the Cromerian

– a succession of several warm stages immediately preceding the Anglian glaciation (see **Table 2**). Although there is currently some debate over the age of the Cromerian, many people now believe that the end of this complex equates with OIS 13 of the deep ocean record. If correctly interpreted this implies that hominids first entered Britain between about 524,000 and 478,000 years ago.

Westbury-sub-Mendip

The site is an enormous collapsed cavern located on the southern edge of the Mendip Hills in Somerset. The cave deposits are exposed on the north-east face of a large open quarry (**31**) and were investigated between 1976 and 1982 by a team from the Natural History Museum. The main chamber of the cave and a large side

30 Map of early fossil hominid sites (skulls) and archaeological sites (open circles) in Europe. Site names: 1 Boxgrove, 2 Kent's Cavern, 3 Westbury-sub-Mendip, 4 High Lodge, 5 Barnham, 6 Swanscombe, 7 Schöningen, 8 Heidelberg, 9 Steinheim, 10 Arago, 11 Atapuerca, 12 Orce, 13 Isernia la pineta, 14 Ceprano.

31 Westbury-sub-Mendip (Somerset). View of excavations conducted by the Natural History Museum in this vast limestone quarry.

chamber contain a considerable depth of deposit, over 30m (100ft) thick. The upper units of the sequence are made up of brecciated (cemented) sands, silts and clays which are richly fossiliferous, containing abundant bones of extinct mammals, small vertebrates and birds. Until recently, evidence for human occupation was regarded as highly conjectural because of the altered appearance of the lithic finds. However, unpublished re-analysis of material recovered from the pink breccia (Unit 11) has shown them to be artefacts of a coarse Greensand Chert that are unquestionably of human manufacture. They include flakes of a non-Acheulian (mode 1) industry. Further signs of early human presence at the site come from a cut-marked bone recovered in Unit 18 of the main chamber. The significance of these artefacts is that they derive from units which can be dated on biostratigraphic evidence to the middle of the Cromerian.

Kent's Cavern

Situated on the west flank of the Ilsham Valley in Torquay, Devon, this famous limestone cave has a long and distinguished history of archaeological exploration extending back to the 1820s (**32**). The earliest deposits with evidence of human activity were investigated by William Pengelly in a sixteen-year programme of excavations which began in 1865. Among the most important finds were Acheulian handaxes (mode 2 industry) recorded in breccia deposits underlying a crystalline stalagmite floor in the inner half of the cave (**33**). More recent work by Chris Proctor, a cave sedimentologist, suggests that the finds were probably introduced by mud flows from the surface rather than by people actually living inside the cave.

Uranium series dating implies that the crystalline stalagmite is over 350,000 years old and is certainly much younger than the underlying breccia in which the artefacts were found. Based on the comparisons of fossil microfauna and the presence of species such as *Homotherium latidens* (a dirk-tooth cat known to have become extinct in the Anglian glaciation),

32 South entrance to Kent's Cavern (Devon).
The illustration shows William Pengelly, one of the
early excavators of the cave.

the breccia has been estimated as being of pre-
Anglian or possibly early Anglian age.

High Lodge

This open-air site excavated by the British
Museum in 1962–8 and 1988 is situated in the
Breckland close to Mildenhall in Suffolk. A
schematic section through the deposits (**34**)
shows a series of silts and clays infilling a stream
channel. The channel sequence is sandwiched
between two glacial 'till' deposits believed to be
of the same Anglian stage. Although the history
of emplacement is complicated, it seems likely
that the silts and clays belong to the end of the
Cromerian Interglacial and were then
subsequently rafted in as a wedge by the
advancing Anglian ice sheet. Pollen and insect
remains from the silts and clays indicate cool
temperate conditions, consistent with a late
interglacial stage. The discovery of a molar of
Stephanorhinus hundsheimensis, a rhino which

33 Handaxes from Kent's Cavern. Right: from the *in situ*
breccia underlying a stalagmite dating to 350,000
years ago. Left: three views of a tool from a disturbed
context but probably of about the same age.

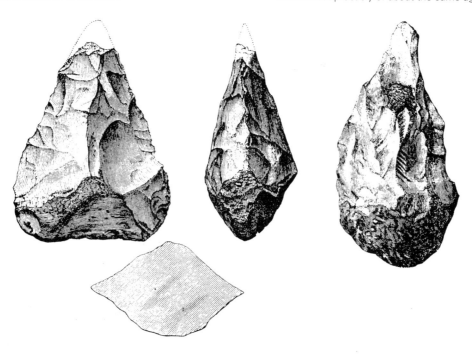

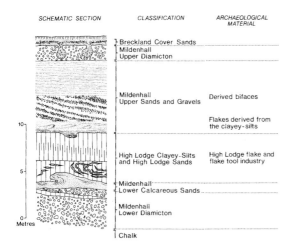

became extinct in the Anglian, also supports the idea that the deposits were formed in a temperate stage before the main Anglian glaciation.

Artefacts found in the clayey silts are arguably of a non-Acheulian (mode 1) industry with finely made side scrapers (**colour plate 5**) and so-called flaked flakes (**35**). The lithic assemblage exhibits certain parallels with the non-handaxe industry at Clacton. However, Acheulian handaxes have been found in the past in a similar stratigraphic position (see **34** and **35**) at the site and in consequence some people have tried to argue that the artefact

34 High Lodge (Suffolk). Schematic section through the archaeological deposits with evidence of handaxes and an underlying flake industry. The sediments of both artefact groups are believed to be of pre-Anglian age.

35 High Lodge retouched tools. Top left, clockwise: a flake scraper and two 'flaked' flakes, and three views of a handaxe.

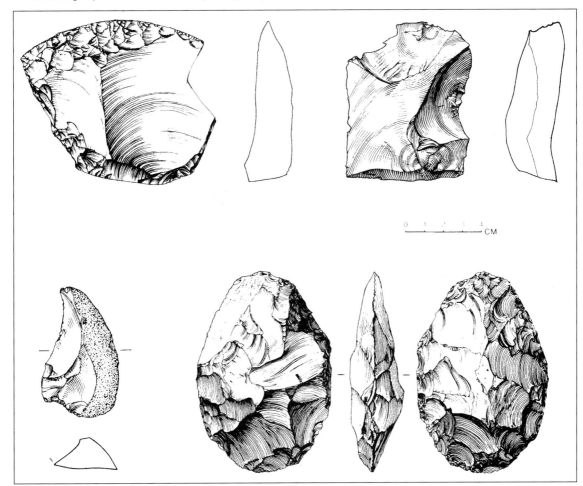

assemblages are, in fact, different parts of the same industry. Although the contemporaneity of the finds layers is still in doubt, it is nevertheless interesting that representatives of both mode 1 (Westbury-sub-Mendip) and mode 2 (Boxgrove, Kent's Cavern) industries do indeed occur in the earliest archaeological record of Britain.

In summary, this chapter has dealt with the earliest hominid settlement of Britain and Europe. Stone artefacts, the most durable items of early prehistoric cultures, provide the most telling evidence of human presence in these regions. According to recent estimates the earliest colonization of northern Europe can be dated to around 500,000 years ago, but this may have lagged significantly behind Spain and the rest of southern Europe. For this early Palaeolithic period in Britain the dating of sites is extremely difficult and depends heavily on the interpretation of biological fossils in association with artefacts. Together they provide a relative dating scheme which allows sites to be fitted into successive warm interglacial or cold glacial stages of the marine isotope record. Now that we have discussed the timing of colonization, we shall focus next on the nature of human occupation and, in particular, on one of the most spectacular Palaeolithic sites in Britain.

4
On the track of our early human ancestors in Britain

Until recently, a chapter on this subject might have been dominated by a dry discussion of stone tool typology, coupled with a few detailed descriptions of geological sections. But, fuelled by fresh discoveries and new methodological approaches, we now have much more exciting ways of investigating the past. Part of the reason for this improving picture is the wave of advances generated by the discovery and excavation of the site of Boxgrove in West Sussex. It is no exaggeration that the investigation of this site since 1985 has quite literally overturned our thinking on the Palaeolithic. Using Boxgrove as a case study, we shall examine in this chapter such questions as: the identity of the earliest inhabitants; what they looked like; how they lived; what they ate; and even their capacity for thought and language. All of these topics impinge upon human social behaviour and vividly bring to life the fossil record in ways that were not previously possible.

Boxgrove: the oldest human remains in Britain

Currently the oldest human remains in Britain come from the Eartham Pit close to the village of Boxgrove, in the West Sussex Downs. The site (already known for its stone artefacts and butchered bones) was discovered as the result of commercial quarrying operations. Apart from the preservation of human remains, the site is uniquely important because its layers are undisturbed (36). The fine-grained sediments

built up fairly rapidly and, because the ground surface was enveloped gently, the artefact and bone scatters lie almost exactly where they were dropped. The site therefore provides a rare record of human activities and a singular opportunity to peer back into the remoter recesses of the past.

Until the Boxgrove discoveries were made it was not even certain whether humans had lived in Britain so long ago. The first of the hominid fossils came to light in the winter of 1993 when Roger Pedersen exposed a large human shin bone (37) in undisturbed deposits near the base of the quarry. Curiously, the bone, a tibia from the left leg, was found on its own, but the fact that it showed animal chew marks suggests it was scavenged by a wolf-size animal. Apart from its good condition, one of the most surprising aspects of the fossil was its large size; it clearly belonged to an individual as tall as a fully grown modern adult yet it came from deposits over 480,000 years old. The tibia was followed in the summer of 1995 by another important fossil discovery of two human front teeth (38). As they were found 90cm (3ft) below the tibia it is clear they are from an earlier stratigraphic unit, but the time difference separating the two fossils can only be surmised. Wear facets on the teeth show conclusively that they would fit together and therefore belonged to one person.

From these few fragmentary remains it is possible to reconstruct fairly accurately what the whole skeleton must have looked like. This is

36 Boxgrove handaxe and bone scatter under excavation.

achieved by comparing the bones and teeth to other fossil skeletons and by using bone length to thickness ratios on modern equivalents. As a result, the length of the Boxgrove tibia shaft (294mm/11.5in) in combination with its thickness can be used to estimate that its owner was about 1.8m (6ft) tall and weighed just over 80kg (12.5 stones). Based on the overall sturdiness of the bone its owner was almost certainly male and must have been fairly muscular.

Both the shin bone and the teeth can provide significant clues about early human lifestyles.

The most obvious feature of the tibia is that it is exceptionally thick walled and robust, much thicker than the shins of modern people. Features of this kind indicate that the bone had to withstand enormous pressures and extremely heavy usage: one implication is that these archaic humans were not spending much time at rest during the day but were constantly busy, moving around. According to palaeoanthropologist Chris Stringer, who is studying the material, only very high levels of activity would produce this

37 Boxgrove hominid tibia, broken at both ends and with signs of carnivore damage.

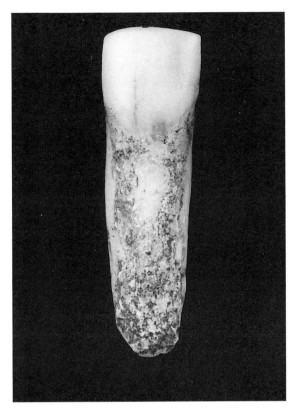

38 Boxgrove hominid lower incisor.

level of cortical thickness. The closest analogy today may be found in marathon runners where the legs develop slightly thicker bones to resist fatigue. The evidence seems to point to the fact that the Boxgrove people lived physically demanding lives.

Information on age, health and diet is potentially available from the teeth and bone, though no results have yet been published for Boxgrove. Estimation of the individual's age is relatively straightforward and would come from osteon growth patterns in the tibia; the degree of wear present on the teeth may also give vital clues. The presence of calculus (tartar) around the base of the incisors can provide evidence of health and diet. The build-up of minerals on the surface of teeth is extremely useful because it traps food residues and mouth bacteria. Recent dental studies have shown that populations with a higher dietary intake of meat protein, such as the Arctic Inuit (eskimo), are more prone to this

condition. In the case of Boxgrove it might also be possible to investigate the question of diet by analyzing the bone chemistry of the tibia, since the rough balance of meat, fish and vegetable foods eaten leaves chemical signatures in the form of detectable carbon and nitrogen isotope ratios.

One other interesting piece of information about the Boxgrove people comes from minute scratches across the face of the incisors. The damage was definitely incurred in the lifetime of the individual because tiny sand and grit particles are embedded in the cut surfaces. According to Mark Roberts, leader of the Boxgrove Project, the diagonal scratches were produced by a sharp flint edge, and are identical to those found on animal bones at the site. A fascinating insight into how the marks might have been made is provided by observing the eating habits of living peoples, some of whom actually slice meat close to the mouth using the teeth to anchor one end of the piece of food. In this position its not hard to imagine frequent contact between the knife blade and the enamel surfaces, resulting in damage to the teeth (see **61**). Similar lesions have also been noticed on the front teeth of later human fossils, such as the Neanderthals, but here the incisors are much more heavily worn, indicating that the mouth was not only used for gripping objects but probably also as a 'tool' for preparing and softening animal hides. Interestingly, the direction of cut-marks from top left to bottom right on the Boxgrove specimens is consistent with the owner being right-handed.

A distant relative or a direct ancestor?

Despite being broken at both ends, the shape and size of the tibia can be used to compare and relate the Boxgrove specimen to those of other European, Asian and African fossils currently placed in the species *Homo heidelbergensis*. Among the best-known representatives of these archaic humans are a lower jaw bone (and type fossil for the species) discovered in 1907 in the Mauer sand quarry, near Heidelberg, Germany, and a skull found in 1960 at Petralona (**39**),

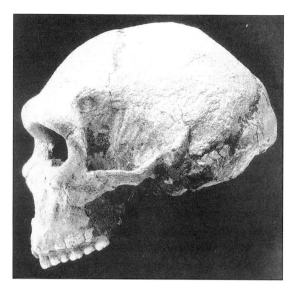

39 Cranium of *Homo heidelbergensis* from Petralona, Greece.

near Thessalonika, eastern Greece. Outside Europe other members of this group are represented by a skull and post-cranial bones from the site of Broken Hill Mine, Kabwe, Zambia (formerly referred to as 'Rhodesian Man') in Africa and by a fossil cranium from Dali in Shanxi Province, China.

These early fossils and others like them enable anthropologists to reconstruct a fuller composite picture of what the Boxgrove hominids must have looked like. The Petralona specimen (**39**) shows they had very large jutting faces. The cranium would have been heavily built, with a sloping forehead behind massive, projecting brow ridges. The Petralona specimen has a large cranial capacity of 1,220cc, which falls within the range of both *Homo erectus* (from Beijing) and archaic *Homo sapiens*. Further clues about the facial appearance of *Homo heidelbergensis* come from the Mauer fossil with its heavy, chinless jaw and relatively small modern-sized teeth. Neither of these examples contradicts the impression of extremely strong, large-bodied creatures, sharing some of the physical characteristics of more advanced hominids. At the same time, however, it should be stressed that the Boxgrove

people would have looked rather different from ourselves at least from the neck up. The most apt description for them is 'archaic humans'.

In terms of lineage position, *Homo heidelbergensis* appears to share features in common with both African *Homo erectus/ergaster* and archaic *Homo sapiens*, occupying a more or less physical mid-point between the two. This is the view presently favoured by Chris Stringer who believes that a common population of 'archaic sapiens' existed in Africa and Europe around 500,000 years ago, but that at some later point, perhaps between 300,000 and 200,000 years ago, it split. The result was that the European branch developed into Neanderthals, while the African branch eventually gave rise to modern humans. The main question is whether Boxgrove (and other fossils like it) can be placed before or after the split. According to Stringer, *Homo heidelbergensis* displays some characteristics which foreshadow those of Neanderthals, but they are still too generalized to be certain. He therefore places Boxgrove before the divergence. An alternative idea held by some Spanish anthropologists is that populations living in Europe 500,000 years ago had already developed distinctive Neanderthal characteristics. If they are right then the Boxgrove people are not our true ancestors but belong instead to the line that evolved into Neanderthals (**40**).

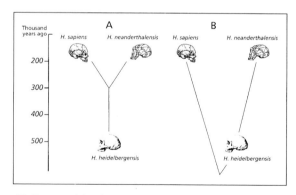

40 Two models of the ancestral relationships between *Homo heidelbergensis* and later European fossil hominids A) as the direct ancestor of the Neanderthals; B) as a common ancestor of both modern humans and Neanderthals.

41 General view of the excavations at Boxgrove (West Sussex).

Whatever the existing uncertainties about the lineage position of *Homo heidelbergensis*, it seems indisputable that the Boxgrove people and African archaic humans had common origins. Evidence for shared ancestry comes, quite literally, in the shape of the human body. As in all early hominids, characteristics of body framework appear to be closely linked to the temperature regimes of the environments in which they lived. In other words, the body's shape is moulded by climate. Nearer the equator people tend to be tall and thin so that heat can be easily dissipated; nearer the poles the bodies are squatter to conserve heat. The Neanderthals (who will be discussed in Chapters 5 and 6) are a good illustration of the latter; their bodies were generally rounder with relatively short limbs to reduce heat loss. But in this respect the Boxgrove people were totally different from Neanderthals: they were much more massively built. It is this heavyweight robustness of the Boxgrove humans that indicates a body reasonably well-adapted to life in northern

climates, but retaining some archaic traits of their more southerly origin such as longer limbs. This would, of course, be wholly consistent with the model suggesting dispersal out of Africa. It would also suggest that Boxgrove provides a logical link between the tall African early humans and the smaller, more robust populations of Neanderthals who subsequently inhabited Britain and Eurasia.

A window on a buried landscape

Looking at the Eartham quarry today, set below the gently rolling South Downs countryside, it is hard to imagine how dramatically this landscape has been transformed over the past 500,000 years. Currently, the site is deeply buried under a vast mantle of chalky gravels 20m (65ft) thick (**41**), but hundreds of thousands of years ago – when the area was occupied by archaic humans – the exposed land surface would have looked entirely different, with the sea only a stone's throw away. Our ability to 'read' the successive changes in the landscape comes from our knowledge of the processes which helped to form the thick layers of geological deposits. Information obtained from vertebrate fossils, pollen, molluscs and charcoal found in the geological sediments can help to fill in the missing environmental details and recreate the landscape, although not all these sources of evidence are present at Boxgrove.

Geological sections visible in the quarry pit reveal a series of layers which cumulatively reflect a full interglacial–glacial cycle (**42**). Evidence of human activities occurs more or less throughout the whole geological sequence. The fact that the sequence is so well preserved is due to various natural processes: erosional forces have ensured that the layers have been buried, sometimes extremely quickly and tectonic movements may also have uplifted the whole

area so that today it lies 43m (141ft) above present sea level. Certainly, uplift seems to have prevented subsequent high interglacial seas from affecting the Boxgrove deposits.

The Boxgrove sequence begins with a series of beach deposits. They accumulated on a platform cut at the base of the South Downs by a warm interglacial sea, probably not much higher than present sea-level. The action of the waves formed a steep cliff, up to 80m (260ft) high, similar to those seen along Britain's south coast today at places like Beachy Head. Immediately below the cliffs a shingle beach developed, but to the south thick layers of marine sands were deposited, known as the Slindon Sands (named after a local village).

Above the sands there are signs of local cliff collapse and the sediments become siltier. Analysis shows that during this period a tidal lake or lagoon formed, cut-off from the sea by a low sandbank or shingle bar. As the climate began to cool and sea-levels dropped slightly, the lagoon silted up and the exposed coastal plain became a wetland habitat of mudflats and

42 Cross-section through the Boxgrove deposits with the main geological sub-divisions. The human figure shown near the base gives an idea of the vertical scale.

Geological Sequence at Boxgrove

— Periglacial Gravel

— Land surface ⎤
⎟ Slindon Silts
— Lagoon Deposits ⎦

— Cliff Collapse ⎤
⎟
⎟
⎟ Slindon Sands
— Marine & Beach Deposits ⎟
⎟
— Tail of Beach ⎦
— Chalk Bedrock

grassland. It is during this phase in the Slindon Silts that the first palpable signs of hominid activity can be definitely traced.

The next stage is represented by a period of stability when a soil formed on the silts. According to faunal data and pollen remains, the landscape must have been relatively open at this stage, dominated by grassland and intermittently dotted with small freshwater springs (near the cliffline). These habitats supported rich communities of grazing herbivores and other animals (43). The existence of freshwater pools also created suitable habitats for waterfowl (Bewick swan, greylag geese, mallard, teal, moorhen), amphibians (frogs and newts) and fish (stickleback). The cliffs overlooking the flats were probably forested at this time, as indicated by the presence of typical woodland animals (wood mouse, hazel dormouse, red squirrel and fallow deer) and songbirds (robin and starling) that prefer woodland scrub.

For archaic humans living in such environments there would no doubt have been ample feeding opportunities, with the added benefits of freely available drinking water from springs, as well as excellent flint sources for toolmaking in the nearby cliff tumble. It was, of course, somewhere in this ancient landscape that one of the Boxgrove hominids finally met his death. The body must have been left unburied as the corpse was later ravaged by one or more carnivores. The gnawed and discarded shin bone eventually came to rest near a small freshwater pool and became naturally incorporated in the surrounding sediments.

The end of the interglacial cycle was signalled by a progressive drop in sea-level as the climate grew steadily drier and cooler. Periglacial deposits overlying the Slindon Silts testify to a worsening of climate causing the downland to erode and cover the lower sediments in chalk and gravels. Intriguingly, fresh-looking flint artefacts have been recovered from within the periglacial gravel showing that archaic humans had not abandoned the area altogether and were able to survive even as the climate noticeably deteriorated.

43 Interglacial fauna represented in the different levels at Boxgrove. Top left, clockwise: lion, rabbit, brown bear, wolf, wild horse, giant deer, fallow deer, hyena, badger, beaver, extinct rhino, wild cat, hedgehog and red squirrel (not to scale).

It is clear then that even during the relatively short geological timespan under consideration (probably no more than 10,000 years), the landscape at Boxgrove changed successively from a marine margin environment to a more open coastline before developing into a lagoonal phase, followed by a temperate open grassland and finally a cold, treeless periglacial tundra, distant from any coastal influences. The sequence thus records a cycle of change through a warm temperate interglacial episode into an ensuing cold stage, consisting of a succession of sediments containing evidence of human activities. The layers of gravel and other sediments, some 15–20m (50–65ft) thick, which finally buried the site also served to protect the palaeo-landscape until quarrying activities in the twentieth century revealed their existence.

Dating Boxgrove

Artefacts and other archaeological evidence at Boxgrove have been recovered from all the major geological units of the interglacial/glacial sequence (see **42**). As no direct means of dating the finds is currently available, establishing the age of the site rests on 'fitting' the Boxgrove sequence into the existing Pleistocene framework using comparative geological and biostratigraphic indicators.

Geological information shows that the interglacial deposits (Slindon Silts and below) are buried under an enormous depth of gravel and chalk rubble left by periglacial activity. The last time conditions were severe enough to produce these effects on such a scale in this part of Britain was in the Anglian cold stage when ice sheets extended as far south as Upminster in north London. Exactly where one places the Anglian glaciation in the overall timescale is still a topic of debate, but many leading experts would now agree that the best match for this cold stage is OIS 12 of the marine isotopic record (see Chapter 2). If verified, this means that the main part of the Boxgrove interglacial sequence belongs to the preceding warm stage (OIS 13), conventionally placed between about 524,000–478,000 years ago. However, a dissenting view put forward by the geologist David Bowen correlates the warm stage at Boxgrove with OIS 11 on the basis of amino acid racemization ratios of marine molluscs. This would make the site considerably younger than most people now currently accept (see **Table 2**).

To provide a solution to these problems palaeontologists have turned to another source of dating evidence which depends on pinpointing evolutionary changes in selected small mammal species. This biological method is sometimes referred to as the 'vole clock' and is based on the idea that evolutionary events can be used as time markers. Voles are particularly useful in this respect because as a group they are highly sensitive to environmental changes and in the past evolved extremely rapidly in response

Table 6

Selected fossil mammals of Boxgrove Interglacial type.

Extinct shrews	*Sorex runtonensis*
	Sorex savinii
Extinct voles	*Pliomys episcopalis*
	Arvicola terrestris cantiana
	Microtus gregalis
Extinct wolf	*Canis lupus mosbachensis*
Extinct spaeloid bear	*Ursus deningeri*
Extinct rhino	*Stephanorhinus hundsheimensis*
Extinct giant deer	*Megaloceros dawkinsi*

to them. One of these major climatic events seems to have taken place in the period around 600,000 years ago when the European grasslands expanded enormously and voles had to adjust to the new conditions or face extinction. In this situation, natural selection tended to favour those voles equipped with continuously growing, high back teeth for processing their food. In other words the numbers of animals with rooted teeth – the early voles (*Mimomys savinii*) – gradually disappeared from the record in favour of the rootless genus *Arvicola*. At Boxgrove, there are no early voles and the rootless watervoles (*Arvicola*) are fairly primitive in appearance, which means they date to just after the evolutionary transition. On the basis of biostratigraphic comparisons with other European and British sites, the best time fit for this grade of evolved vole would be with the warm stage OIS 13.

Some support for this scheme is provided by fossil evidence of other mammal species present in the Boxgrove fauna. Using the same framework of animals and interglacials (see Chapter 2) it can be shown that all of the species found in Currant's Group 4 are also common to Boxgrove. From the 'mammal signature' it is clear that Boxgrove belongs to an interglacial at the end of the Cromerian Complex, thus strengthening the case for a

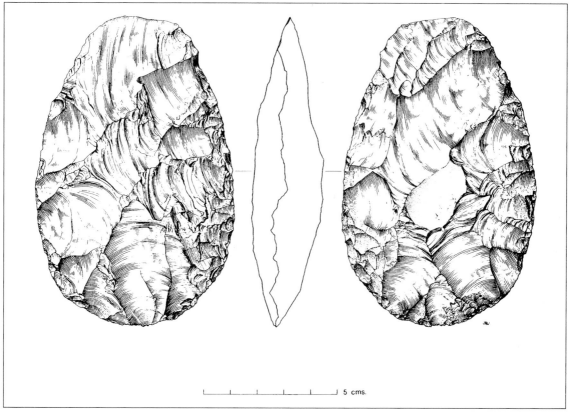

44 Boxgrove ovate handaxe.

pre-Anglian age. In addition to animals familiar to us in the present interglacial (see **23** and **43**), the Boxgrove fauna includes many extinct species (**Table 6**).

Tools and toolmaking at Boxgrove

The majority of stone implements at Boxgrove are bifacially flaked handaxes which come in a variety of shapes from ovate (**44**) to more pointed forms (**45**). In 1995 over 150 of these types were recovered from one small area of the site alone. Pointed handaxe forms are generally much less numerous over the site as a whole. In the past, it had been assumed that the shape of handaxes evolved over time from pointed types into ovates and other related forms. Now however, such ideas on typological progression have been largely discredited due in part to sites like Boxgrove, where both variants are found alongside one another and in the same stratigraphic units. A much more likely

explanation is that shape is influenced by the quality of the raw material available. At Boxgrove the basic oval shape, even in the oldest layers, seems to be the universally preferred form. But it is noticeable that where there is a drop in quality of raw material there is an increase in the thicker pointed handaxe forms (**45**).

45 Pointed and ovate handaxes from contemporary deposits at Boxgrove.

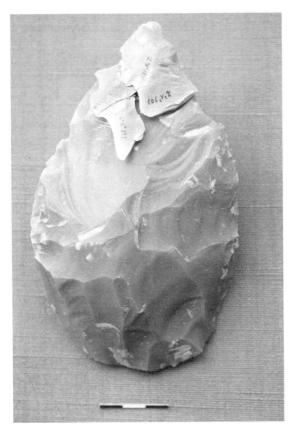

46 Boxgrove ovate handaxe with refitting tranchet thinning flakes.

47 Boxgrove flintknapping scatter in undisturbed condition. It measures about 25cm (10in) across.

Much of the archaeology relates to the manufacture and use of handaxes. Represented across the site are all the various stages of production from the selection and testing of raw material, through the entire knapping procedure in which the flint nodules were first flaked into ovates and finished or thinned by oblique (tranchet) blows at one end (see **2** and **46**). Episodes of re-sharpening and refining the handaxes are also documented, as well as the final discard of used (and sometimes unused) handaxes. In a number of areas of the site, due to quite remarkable preservation, waste material lies almost exactly where it was flaked. By refitting this waste it is possible to work out how the tools were made. The presence of large anvil and hammerstones and experimental flaking show that the first stages in manufacturing the Boxgrove handaxes frequently involved the use of dense stone hammers. Flakes detached in this way often exhibit distinct characteristics (see **4**). A later stage in the process involved the thinning of the tools and this again leaves characteristic features on the waste flakes. One of the many remarkable finds at the site is a small flint scatter consisting of both primary and thinning flakes (**47**). From the shape of the scatter – which forms a tight nest of flakes less than 25cm (10in) across – it is clear that the knapper sat on the

48 Modern flintknapping experiments by Chris Bergman reveal similarities with the undisturbed Boxgrove flint scatters.

that the Boxgrove people had considerable technological abilities. The likelihood that other types of 'soft' hammers also existed is indicated by animal long bones that have percussion marks at their ends; but wooden hammers, if they were used at all, have not survived.

Other than handaxes, tools are relatively rare. At present a total of about twenty recognizable flake tools such as side-scrapers, end-scrapers and various related notched and transverse types are known from the entire site. Apart from these formal tools, a few other artefacts show signs of minor modification linked to blunting or edge-straightening. The obvious contrast in the frequency of handaxes to other tools is also highlighted by numerous waste flakes identified in connection with biface reduction, thinning and re-sharpening work (see **46**). These pieces demonstrate unequivocally that handaxes were the central object of flaking activity.

Food, glorious food

The main dietary evidence comes from large numbers of bones which litter the site. In many cases concentrations of cut bones are actually associated with stone artefacts, thereby providing a direct link with human activities. Some of the bone scatters contain the fossilized remains of single animals such as horse and

ground with the hammer held in one hand and the flint nodule in the other (**48**), with struck waste dropping into his lap. Refitting by Louise Austin, one of the Boxgrove Project workers, has shown that a handaxe was made and presumably carried to another part of the site since the tool itself was missing from the scatter.

A further glimpse into the manufacturing methods used at the site has been provided by the discovery of a beam of deer antler, heavily abraded at one end. Previously the existence of 'soft' bone and antler hammers had been predicted by features on some of the finishing flakes (see **4**), but no definite proof existed. However, in late 1995 – from the same area as the concentration of over 150 handaxes – the base of an antler was found with small chips of flint embedded in its surface (**49**). The find shows it was used to strike flint and confirms

49 Red deer antler hammer from Boxgrove, more than 15cm (6in) long. The degree of wear on the crown (right-hand side) suggests this tool was used to make a large number of handaxes.

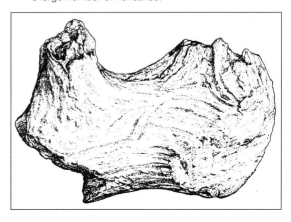

rhino and provide an extraordinary insight into the methods of food-getting and preparation, as well as patterns of meat consumption. The absence of other potential foodstuffs, such as plant remains, does not of course mean that these were not eaten. Such organic items are extremely fragile and rarely survive in the fossil record. Also it seems quite likely, according to the excavators, that meat-on-the-bone was transported away from the stench and debris of the processing areas. If they are right, then a likely destination may have been the wooded areas of downland overlooking the site. In addition to offering secure sleeping places, these habitats would have been rich in berries, roots, fungi and edible plant foods. The lack of hearths or burnt bone at Boxgrove does not preclude the possibility that fires or roasting pits were made on the woodland edge, closer to accessible fuel sources.

GTP 17 Horse Butchery site: a snapshot in time

One of the most informative locations at Boxgrove is area GTP 17. Here, excavations in 1989 and 1991 revealed the remains of a large horse skeleton with several discrete piles of waste flakes scattered around it. The excellent condition of the bones allowed a detailed study to be made of the bone surfaces, while the undisturbed nature of the flints led to refitting work. By piecing together the flint flakes it was possible to prove that several handaxes had been manufactured on the spot, yet intriguingly, the tools themselves were missing. How were the archaeologists able to reconstruct events at this site?

According to Mark Roberts and Simon Parfitt, chief investigators of the project, the site casts a unique spotlight on the behaviour of archaic humans: specifically, it shows how the horse died and how it was then expertly dismembered and butchered to obtain meat, internal organs and other edible tissues (50). Incisions on the bones (51), left by flint tools, indicate how the animal carcass was successively skinned, disarticulated and defleshed. Following this treatment some of the bones, including the lower margin of the horse jaw, were smashed open using large hammerstones. The insides of bones provide rich sources of bone marrow and this together with the organs and other softer tissues, such as the tongue, seem to have been highly prized by the occupants of the site.

Even though no handaxes were found at GTP 17, it is virtually certain they were the prime

50 Artist's reconstruction of Boxgrove showing speared foal and flintknappers in left foreground.

51 A fragment of a horse's pelvis with cut-marks.

butchery tools for skinning, boning and jointing carcasses. The reasons for believing this are based on the results of functional studies: making and using experimental replicas and analyzing the Boxgrove handaxes themselves for use-wear traces. The use of handaxes as butchery tools is by no means a new suggestion. They have sometimes been referred to as the original all-purpose 'Swiss Army Knives' of the Palaeolithic. In addition to their long, sharp cutting edge, usually extending around the whole perimeter, the variety of edge angles also offered possibilities for scraping, slicing and related actions. The all-in-one nature of the ovates is superbly illustrated in the Boxgrove examples by the combination of strong cutting edges and a razor-thin flake edge at one end made by careful finishing (see **46**).

John Mitchell, a microwear specialist, has made an in-depth study of the handaxes from Boxgrove. Using high-power microscopes he has been able to observe in great detail the edges of the tools and to compare them with identical examples used experimentally to cut through animal hide and meat (**colour plate 6**). In one of his experiments he gave several ovate handaxe replicas to a local butcher to deflesh and joint a deer carcass. The butcher, who had never used stone tools before, found them extremely effective for cutting and slicing through skin and flesh. The advantage over other tools, such as small flakes, seemed clear: the handaxe was comfortable to hold, its continuous curved edge

stayed remarkably sharp and offered a wide variety of edge types for carving and slicing. It was also much less slippery to use in the hand than a single flake.

Interestingly, the only task for which the handaxe seemed curiously deficient was in cutting bone. Experimental observation suggests that activities involving the disarticulating of ribs or vertebra were probably undertaken using a combination of scoring and snapping the bone.

As if to underline the positive nature of the tool-use experiments, Mitchell was later able to demonstrate that, like their modern counterparts, the Boxgrove handaxes had evidently been used over much of their circumference (**52**). He was able to match clearly the use-wear on the archaeological pieces to that produced in the butchery experiments. Whether or not the small flakes produced in biface manufacture were themselves used as tools is still unclear. According to the preliminary results it seems that apart from handaxe re-sharpening flakes relatively few other artefacts appear to carry wear traces. Certainly none of the waste flakes from GTP 17 seem to have been extensively utilized.

Some of the most controversial ideas about the horse butchery site concern the method by which the animal was killed. Up until now there has been widespread debate as to whether or not archaic humans were active hunters or passive scavengers relying on other carnivores to do the

52 Low magnification close-up of a meat polish on one of the Boxgrove handaxes.

killing for them. The Boxgrove investigators believe that direct evidence for hunting is provided by the horse's broken shoulder blade, which has a neat semi-circular hole through it. According to Bernard Knight, one of Britain's leading pathologists, the penetrative wound shows all the signs of having been caused by moderately high speed impact with a moving object. Using experimental techniques it has been possible to show that similar damage is caused by a sharpened wooden stave smashing into the side of an animal. And this has led to the speculation that simple spears might have been used to hunt animals the size of rhino and horse 500,000 years ago.

No traces of wooden hunting spears have yet been found at Boxgrove, but Mark Roberts recognizes important parallels in the Clacton spear (found earlier this century in waterlogged deposits thought to be 400,000 years old) and recently discovered objects from Schöningen in Lower Saxony (Germany). Here, up to seven straight spears about 2m (6½ft) long have been found, sharpened at one end (**colour plate** 7), along with a much shorter shaft pointed at both ends. The spears are each made of individual trunks of tough spruce wood, and their centre of gravity is closer to the tip end, as in modern javelins. Interestingly, ethnographic examples of similar spears are known today from East Africa where the Masai use them for hunting rhino. There are no obvious explanations for the shorter length of wood; it may have been a resharpened fragment of a broken spear since it is also made of spruce. Alternatively, some people have suggested affinities with simple throwing sticks. On this evidence, there can be little doubt that the manufacture of efficient hunting spears was well advanced even at this early stage of hominid development.

Before leaving GTP 17, it should be emphasized that although seven separate knapping episodes can be recognized, no handaxes were recovered at the site. The implication seems reasonably clear: after the horse was butchered, the handaxes were deliberately removed, presumably carried away for a similar activity elsewhere. In itself, this one event may not seem particularly remarkable, but in overall terms it suggests a surprisingly flexible pattern of behaviour. Handaxes were not just being made for immediate use but were being 'curated' for a planned future purpose. As we shall see below this raises a number of interesting issues which will be used to challenge some of the more traditional views concerning archaic human behaviour.

Archaic humans and lifestyles: the broader issues

A fifteen-minute culture?

So far in this book there has been an implicit assumption that archaic hominids like those at Boxgrove were merely less advanced versions of ourselves and thus theoretically capable of some forms of modern behaviour. Opinions on this subject, however, are deeply divided. An alternative view, put forward by Clive Gamble, one of Britain's leading palaeolithic experts, is that the Boxgrove people were much more primitive – in some ways hardly more advanced than their tool-assisted distant ancestors in Africa. Among the key progressive elements lacking in their repertoire were the intellectual capabilities necessary for sophisticated language and the ability to plan and think ahead. Though technologically efficient, the lifestyles of these archaic humans were based around their immediate needs: obtaining protein by opportunistic scavenging and gaining access to meaty carcasses with the assistance of stone tools. There was no hunting, there were no long-term storage facilities and artefacts were made primarily for tasks immediately to hand. For Gamble the archaeology at Boxgrove bears all the hallmarks of 'a fifteen-minute culture', the work of intellectual inferiors not even halfway up the giant human cognitive beanstalk.

If these views are deliberately provocative, they do at least help focus attention on some of the key issues concerning our modern human origins, and more specifically, on arriving at suitable criteria for differentiating 'advanced' from 'archaic' cultural behaviour. Some potentially relevant criteria are briefly considered below.

Food for thought: hunting and brain development

So far the only direct evidence of hunting at Boxgrove is rather scanty and consists of a horse's shoulder blade with a hole in it, which not everyone accepts as unequivocal proof of deliberate spearing. The alternative view is that the accumulations of animal bones are due entirely to carnivore activity and that archaic humans simply took advantage of the situation by preying on the kills of other predators. In other words, the Boxgrove people were not hunters at all but opportunistic scavengers. This, of course, is much closer to Gamble's view of archaic humans. He argues that a well-equipped group of hominids with sophisticated hunting techniques should not have taken nearly a million years to colonize Europe and other areas of the Old World.

Despite the apparent lack of hard information, many people are now prepared to believe that archaic humans like the Boxgrove people were indeed capable hunters. Spearheading this view, so to speak, is the anthropologist Peter Wheeler, who refers to the size of our brains as indirect evidence of massive improvements in the nutritional quality of archaic human diets. He argues that the brain of early hominids like *Homo erectus* had expanded enormously. This growth in size required huge investments of the body's energy since the brain uses up 20 per cent of all bodily requirements. An interesting discovery is that in all animals there is a correlation between the size of the brain (as well as other organs) and body size. However, when compared to other animals of our size, our brain is 1kg (2.2lb) heavier than anticipated while our digestive tract is 1kg lighter than expected. From this Wheeler concludes that at some time in the past when our brains expanded, our bellies didn't follow suit. He attributes this to a growing dependence on high quality foods such as meat and animal

proteins which allowed the gut to shrink while at the same time freeing up energy to be reallocated to a highly expensive organ like the brain.

This extremely elegant argument predicts a relationship in hominids between brain expansion and a greater reliance on high protein meaty foods. It is only a small step in the argument, as Wheeler has stated, to suggest that the development of sophisticated hunting techniques would ensure a regular and constant supply of meat and other animal proteins to fuel the higher energy requirements.

Returning to Boxgrove, Mark Roberts has pointed out that the potential meat yields from the larger herbivores found at the site would have been enormous. For example, based on the modern Sumatran rhino, the size to meat weight ratios of the Boxgrove animals suggests up to 700kg (1,540lb) of edible products per animal, while a single horse could provide about 400kg (880lb). The combined weight of edible products from just one rhino would therefore provide the weight equivalent to about 6,167 quarter-pound hamburgers. Provided some form of preservation was possible (by air drying or pounding into edible cake form, e.g. pemmican), this amount of meat would certainly be enough to sustain a relatively large group of hominids for several weeks.

It is important then to consider the fact that hominids at Boxgrove were indeed able to obtain the meat from animals the size of fully grown adult rhinos. These are potentially extremely dangerous animals and have no known natural predators among living carnivores. The evidence also suggests that the Boxgrove people were definitely gaining primary access to the carcasses. This is demonstrated by the fact that where cut-marks occur in association with gnaw marks, they invariably underlie them. In other words carnivores were only getting the leftovers after humans had finished with them. Moreover, the location of cut-marks on the skulls demonstrates that the soft parts such as the eyes and tongue were intact when butchery began and this means the kills must have been fresh. Finally, it is interesting that virtually all stages of the butchery process are represented, even down to the smashing of marrow bones, implying uninterrupted and unhurried access to the dead animals. In combination, each of these pieces of evidence suggests that the hominids were complete masters of their situation. Meat from a range of animals, including bison, giant deer and red deer, was relatively easy to obtain using spears; butchery was conducted in a leisurely manner and the choicest packages of meat and muscle were often then removed elsewhere for storage or immediate consumption. All of these factors point to archaic humans being highly successful meat-eating hunters rather than habitual scavengers.

From my own point of view it seems inescapable that hunting arose out of opportunistic scavenging, but after hunting developed it is unlikely that one form of activity excluded the other. In fact it is quite likely that the two methods continued to be practised side by side following seasonal patterns of game availability or as the situation permitted. This is certainly the case today among modern hunter-gatherers like the Hadza of Tanzania where hunting is preferred in the wet season and scavenging during the dry season. Although the seasonal cycles are very different in northern latitudes it is not hard to imagine a situation at Boxgrove whereby game congregated for longer periods around the freshwater pools (in summer perhaps), and dispersed at other times into the wooded interior. Each of these situations may have called for different food-getting strategies and I would suggest that opportunistic scavenging was still very much part of the archaic lifestyle. Unfortunately at Boxgrove no mortality data on the animals are currently available to test these ideas.

Language capacity

Were the archaic humans at Boxgrove capable of spoken language? This is extremely difficult to answer as we still only have the barest details about how language arose in our modern species. For archaeologists, the question is often split into two separate issues demanding slightly different lines of enquiry: first, did archaic humans have the necessary physical apparatus for making complex verbal sounds and, second, had the internal structures of the brain developed sufficiently to allow sophisticated language? Both approaches make use of the very scanty fossil evidence available, but the second also relies on ideas derived from biological theory. Not surprisingly this is a subject on which there is no conclusive agreement, since many of the ideas put forward are still extremely speculative.

Various studies have been made of the fossil imprints of hominid brains (endocranial casts). From the wrinkles on the surface of the brain it has been possible to suggest that Broca's area (53) (the region linked to speech production) was present in early hominids as far back as *Homo habilis*. By inference, therefore, it would be reasonable to suppose that Boxgrove Man had linguistic capabilities. Against this, Philip Lieberman, a speech analyst, has noted that special landmarks on the base of skulls indicative of a modern vocal tract are positioned differently in archaic human fossils. According to him early speech patterns would have been extremely

53 A profile view of the brain showing locations thought to be associated with language production (Broca's area) and comprehension (Wernicke's area).

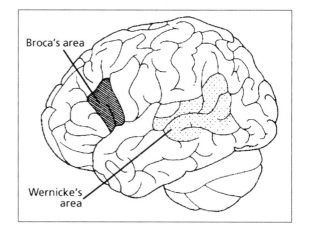

limited without an advanced voice box. This view is supported to some extent by the results of work by physical anthropologist Ann Mclarnon which has shown that muscles in the lower chest of the Nariokotome boy (*Homo ergaster*) were insufficiently developed to make complex speech sounds. Thus the fossil evidence still remains disappointingly ambiguous on the question of speech in early humans, though perhaps veering very slightly towards a negative view.

A completely different angle to the question has been adopted by the anthropologist Robin Dunbar. From a theoretical viewpoint he has proposed a link between optimum group size in primates and the time spent by individuals in social bonding; for chimpanzees and baboons the mechanism for cohesion is grooming. According to this view, social relationships are moderated in primate groups by constant touching and grooming which bonds individuals and cements friendships. Chimps and baboons tend to live in troops of about 50–55 individuals, and about 20 per cent of their waking time is spent in grooming each other. The equivalent social grouping in modern humans has been estimated at roughly 150 individuals, which represents the number of friends and relations that you know well. If the same proportion of time were devoted to grooming in humans this would take up about 40–45 per cent of each day, but it would seriously interfere with the time necessary for other essential activities such as feeding. So, Dunbar has come up with the ingenious idea that language came into being as a method of reinforcing and developing social bonds within these large groups. At the same time it allowed the size of human groups to expand beyond the levels imposed by grooming time budgets.

Of course, the question of when such changes became necessary and people started living in large groups is still fiercely disputed. Nevertheless, it is abundantly clear that the seat of language lies in the complex wiring of the brain. The maintaining and mapping of social relationships would also have been improved by increased brain size. Based on a hypothetical link between brain size and group size, anthropologist Leslie Aiello has estimated that modern speech capabilities did not develop any earlier than about 250,000 years ago, which is of course long after the time of the Boxgrove people.

Thus I think it is fairly safe to conclude that the Boxgrove humans did not have modern patterns of speech vocalization. Moreover, if they had any form of language, it is unlikely to have progressed beyond a prototype stage. Such a view, of course, would not contradict the suggestion that they had a perfectly adequate means of communication – indeed such a tool would be vital in hunting large and dangerous animals such as the rhino, an activity that depended on the cooperation of many individuals.

Stone tools as cognitive markers

Investigating the recesses of the prehistoric mind is not exactly easy since soft tissue does not fossilize, but one promising method of seeing how archaic minds might have ticked is through the study of stone tools. Take for example one of the simplest tools of the stone age: a pebble tool (see 7). To make a unifacial chopper several flakes are removed one after the other from the end of a pebble, producing a sharp cutting edge. Apart from a basic understanding of edge angles and a certain amount of dexterity in striking flakes, little other knowledge is needed, just plenty of practice. The whole procedure may involve three or four blows to the pebble and take a matter of seconds. The simplicity of the technique is underlined by the fact that captive chimpanzees can be trained to reproduce such tools. Now contrast this simple tool with a handaxe, an artefact that requires working on both faces and in such a way as to maintain straight edges and a symmetrical form (both lengthways and sideways). From knapping experiments and refitting studies at Boxgrove and elsewhere it is clear that the manufacturing process is much more complicated. To begin with, it involves an average of fifty or so consecutive flake removals, as well as careful thinning and finishing with soft hammers. Not only does this operation require a high degree of manual dexterity and skill, but the maker has to be able to visualize the final product before it is made. Not surprisingly, perhaps, toolmaking on this scale is well beyond the capabilities of even the most gifted chimpanzees.

What does this tell us about the minds of the Boxgrove knappers? For archaeologists like John Gowlett, the ability to make handaxes marks an important threshold in human cognitive development. It shows that archaic humans had evolved a capacity for memory (i.e. they learnt long flake sequences) and had a more sophisticated awareness of raw materials than their ancestors. At the same time, judging by the extraordinary symmetry and shared likeness of the tools, hominids had attained a sufficient level of mental organization to allow actions to be performed in thought, removing the need for constant trial and error – a concept referred to by psychologists as 'reversibility'. All of this implies that the archaics had developed considerable problem-solving abilities and were able to reflect and act upon stored knowledge. Linked to these advances may have been the ability to engage in 'forward planning'.

At Boxgrove, Mark Roberts believes that some aspects of contingency planning – anticipating future needs – can be demonstrated by the archaeological evidence. In one area of the site, for example, 150 handaxes were found, some clearly unused. Since this was far in excess of the number actually required for butchering the carcasses immediately to hand, he has suggested that the overproduction was either to do with deliberate stockpiling or was based on an overestimate of the numbers of animals that were going to be killed. Seen in this context it is amusing to think that 'blind over-optimism' is not nearly so modern a cultural trait as we might imagine! A second piece of evidence concerns tool 'curation'. This is linked to the idea, originally put forward by Lewis Binford, that items of personal equipment are often carefully maintained by the individual and

rarely thrown away unless broken. Potential examples of personal effects are extremely difficult to recognize in the Palaeolithic record, but the flintknapper's antler hammer found at Boxgrove was possibly just such a piece of equipment. Some effort must have been required in making the tool in the first place (i.e. separating the upper part of the beam), while heavy traces of wear on the base testify to its extensive use probably by a single flintknapper. Apart from these examples, one might also add the fact that handaxes were sometimes made at the raw material source, near the cliff, before being carried 250m (270yd) to the butchery locations. This in itself also implies a certain level of anticipatory behaviour.

A different theoretical approach to the question of human cognition has recently been developed by the archaeologist Steven Mithen. Using the latest ideas on evolutionary and child psychology he has put forward a theory of the modular mind. Here, the mind can be compared to the structure of a medieval cathedral with its central nave and adjoining chapels. He sees the modern mind as comprising a nave of general intelligence connected to multiple chapels of specialized intelligence (each responsible for specific behavioural domains, e.g. technical, linguistic, social). In his proposed three-phase model of evolutionary development, Mithen would characterize archaic human minds (e.g. Boxgrove) as having developed specialized intelligences, but ones that were not fully connected to the nave of generalized intelligence (see **62**). Thus although knowledge of hunting and toolmaking were reasonably advanced, thoughts demanding an interaction of more than one domain, such as designing a custom-made hunting tool for a specific animal, were simply beyond the scope of this grade of hominid. Such a view would seem to have much in common with Clive Gamble's perception that the Boxgrove occupants were undoubtedly well-organized and efficient in the technical and routine matters of food-getting, but were incapable of advanced planning in a modern sense.

Cultural variability in the Lower Palaeolithic
Before leaving Boxgrove altogether it would be worth reminding ourselves that the British Lower Palaeolithic contains evidence of two apparently distinct stone tool industries: mode 1 type (pebble cores and flake tools) as at Westbury-sub-Mendip and Clacton, Essex, and mode 2 type (handaxes) as at Kent's Cavern and Boxgrove. In the past it was assumed that these two technologies represented distinct cultural groupings: an earlier, simpler culture known as the Clactonian and a later one with handaxes known as the Acheulian. At one time it was also believed that the two industries were the product of culturally different peoples, perhaps even completely different hominid lineages. Now, however, as a result of dating sites such as Boxgrove it can be shown that Acheulian industries were at the very least contemporary with Clactonian ones, and may be considerably older.

To explain variation between the Acheulian and Clactonian in the contemporary early Palaeolithic record, Steven Mithen has suggested that the two technologies represent alternative types of archaic human culture. In the Clactonian, the flake making displays a low level of technical skill and this is attributed to small groups living in wooded environments. Because of their relative isolation they came into contact with few other toolmakers and hence technical ability remained rooted in trial-and-error learning. In contrast, following Mithen, the handaxe-makers of the Acheulian operated in much larger groups, living in open tundra habitats with greater opportunities for social intermixing. As a result social learning enabled traditions of more complex toolmaking to be passed on from one generation to the next.

This environmentally centred view of the Clactonian and Acheulian is not shared by all concerned. Flint technology specialists John MacNabb and Nick Ashton, for instance, have made a detailed study of the relevant assemblages and have come to the conclusion that the flakes and flake tools in both industries are made in an identical way. Interestingly, they also now claim to have identified actual examples of handaxes in the Clactonian group. Excavations at one of their sites at Barnham, Suffolk, have produced direct evidence that the Clactonian and Acheulian were closely contemporary. The site consists of gravel deposits on the edge of an ancient river channel (54). Flint obtained from this source was taken to two adjacent areas: in one of them flakes were

54 Barnham (Suffolk). Excavations in progress showing an area of natural cobbles where flakes were manufactured.

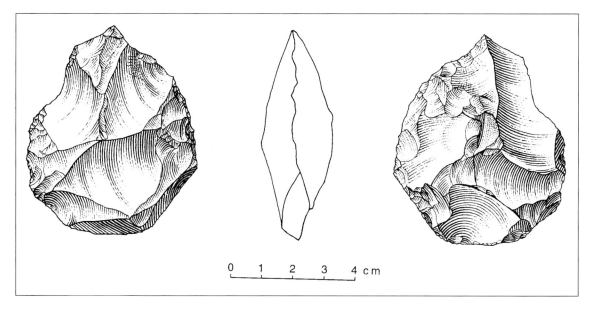

0 1 2 3 4 cm

55 One of the Acheulian handaxes from Barnham.

prepared, while in the other, two or three small handaxes (55) were manufactured. On the basis of this they propose that, far from being deeply seated cultural traditions, the manufacture of different artefacts simply demonstrates a flexible approach to problem-solving in different situations. For example, the handaxes in one area of the site may have been linked to butchery activities, while elsewhere flakes were used in another expedient task. They also point out that at Barnham – as at other Clactonian sites – the raw material is not of particularly good quality being largely unsuitable for making handaxes. So, in their view, the quality of the raw materials exerts an important influence over what gets made.

From my own viewpoint, I would tend to agree with the analysis of MacNabb and Ashton. To begin with, we know that archaic humans were extremely mobile and it is very likely that at Boxgrove, which lay close to woodland, the handaxe-makers deliberately chose to occupy the woodland margin. They could doubtless have slept in the relative safety of the forest and emerged onto the grassland plains for hunting purposes. Thus the particular link made by Mithen, between tool behaviour and social behaviour, seems overcomplicated. There are also sites of contemporary age in Britain and Europe which contradict his model. For example in Germany, mode 1 assemblages can occur in open situations (Miesenheim I), while mode 2 handaxe assemblages (Kärlich-Seeufer) are known from more closed environments. One test of the McNabb–Ashton hypothesis (but not the only one) will be to see if Clactonian toolkits continue to turn up in association with poorer quality raw materials. Inevitably, this will depend on the discovery of new, well-stratified sites to test such theories. But, clearly, for archaeologists working in this period, exciting times lie ahead.

5
The Neanderthals

For a long time Neanderthals have endured mixed reviews in the popular and scientific press: at one extreme is the image of the sub-human, club-wielding brute; and of course, the term 'Neanderthal' itself is still reserved as a form of abuse for people with socially unacceptable or old-fashioned attitudes. At the other extreme is the image of the enlightened flower-children, a view much promoted in the 1960s in the wake of the famous discovery of the garlanded burial at Shanidar Cave in Iraq.

Despite this seemingly paradoxical modern view, it has frequently been observed that the changing image of Neanderthals has more to do with the way we would like to see our human ancestors than with any objective interpretation of the archaeological and fossil evidence. One of the inevitable consequences is that supporters of the idea that Neanderthals were a member of our own species play down any major distinctions between archaic humans and ourselves, while those who view them as only distant evolutionary cousins tend to emphasize the differences.

Before considering the question of behavioural traits and lifestyles in more detail, I shall begin by reviewing the anatomical evidence for Neanderthals, their dating and their origins. In adopting this framework, I am deliberately aiming to separate the biological and the social spheres but, in doing so, I am conscious of the fact that such distinctions are sometimes artificial because the two elements are so closely intertwined. Thus in examining the physical evidence some aspects of Neanderthal behaviour will invariably be included.

Definition

The name itself comes from the Neander Valley (or 'thal') near Düsseldorf in Germany. Here in 1856, human bones and part of a skull were discovered by workmen engaged in building a quarry railway line. The bones came from a natural fissure in the limestone known as the Feldhofer Cave about 18m (30ft) above the river bed, in a thick layer of cave earth. That this momentous discovery was made at all owes a great deal to the activities of a sharp-eyed schoolteacher, Johann Carl Fuhlrott. It was due to his timely intervention that the bones were rescued from the valley slope after they had been unceremoniously dumped by the quarrymen, in the mistaken belief that they were the remains of a cave bear.

Ironically, the Feldhofer individual was not the first of its kind to be discovered. Earlier in the century finds had been made of a fragmentary child's skull at Engis Cave in Belgium in 1829–30, and a partial skull of a female Neanderthal had been uncovered in 1848 in Forbes' Quarry on Gibraltar. Had the scientific significance of either of these finds been recognized, we might now be referring instead to Calpians (after the ancient name for Gibraltar) or Engisians, rather than Neanderthals!

In terms of the geographic distribution of fossils, Neanderthals are found over a very wide area of Europe and western Asia, but not in Africa. Most of the fossil evidence can be shown to date to the period 130,000–30,000 years ago, covering much of the last interglacial/glacial cycle (see **15** and **Table 2**). Neanderthals displaying the most well-developed characteristics of their type are often referred to as 'classic' Neanderthals, and are believed to have evolved in Eurasia in response to the cooler conditions of the last glaciation. The features seen on the type-fossil from Feldhofer Cave (Germany) are typical of those shared by the classic Neanderthals. The term 'pre-Neanderthals' is reserved for fossils earlier than 130,000 years ago but which share certain common traits.

Physical appearance

As a group, Neanderthals are fairly easy to characterize because of the abundant fossils available for study, covering nearly all parts of the skeleton. The fact that many of the bones have survived is principally due to the excellent conditions for preservation in caves, which is where the majority of fossils have been discovered. Yet, despite this wealth of evidence, it is surprising that, historically speaking, there has been so much controversy and disagreement concerning their actual physical appearance.

One of the earliest, most complete skeletons to be studied was discovered in 1908 at the cave of La Chapelle-aux-Saints, in the Dordogne (south-west France). The skeleton was first described by the great French anatomist Marcellin Boule who misinterpreted the effects of old age and disease on the bones and so drew a picture of a very different individual. Despite recognizing the modern size of the brain, the rest of the body seemed primitive by comparison: stoop-shoulders, a curved spine, bowed limbs and restricted leg movements caused by limitations of the knee joints. All of these traits suggested to him a very lowly creature relegated to the margins of human ancestry (**56**). Although such views did not go

unchallenged it was not until almost half a century later that the anatomists William Straus and A. J. E. Cave were formally able to disprove some of Boule's assertions. Re-analysis of the skeleton revealed that the bones were heavily afflicted with arthritis, especially around the joints, and this would have accounted for the ungainly, bent-kneed posture highlighted by Boule. The new work also showed conclusively that Neanderthals not only walked upright but, from a distance, could easily be mistaken for people like ourselves (**57**). Straus and Cave concluded in a now famous throwaway remark that such was the physical similarity with modern humans that, given a shave and a new suit, a Neanderthal could easily 'be reincarnated and placed in a New York subway'.

Thus the Neanderthal image most favoured today is one of a people like us, but nevertheless different. So what exactly are these differences and how would we identify them?

56 Reconstruction (1909) of a Neanderthal based on Marcellin Boule's scientific analysis of the Chapelle-aux-Saints human fossil.

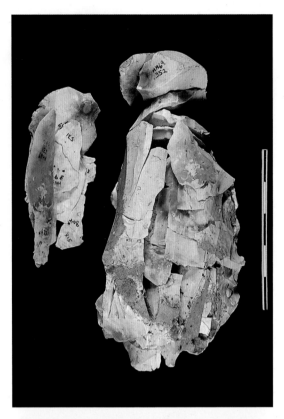

1 Refitted blade core from the Final Upper Palaeolithic site of Hengistbury Head (Dorset). 10cm (4in) scale.

2 Exploded view of the same blade core from Hengistbury Head with ninety flakes and blades. The abandoned core weighed just 193g, as compared to the 710g of the refitted block. Notice also that many of the blades (shown right) accidentally snapped during knapping. The conjoins include one tool, a retouched blade.

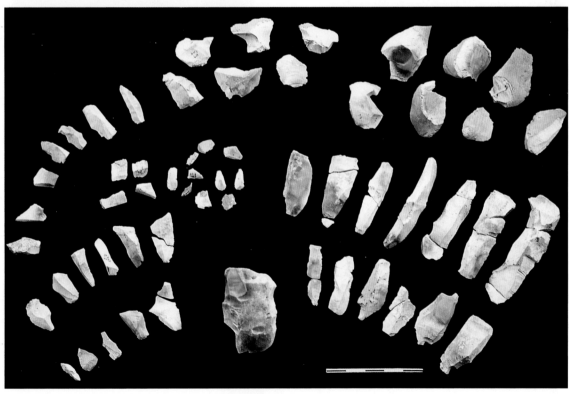

3 Upper Palaeolithic Solutrean laurel leaf point.

4 Fossil hyena jaw. These animals lived all over Europe in the last glaciation and used caves for denning purposes.

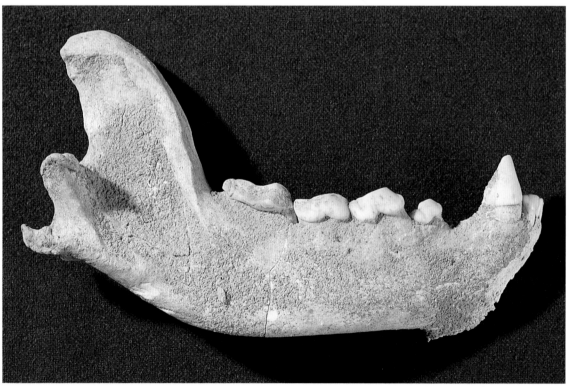

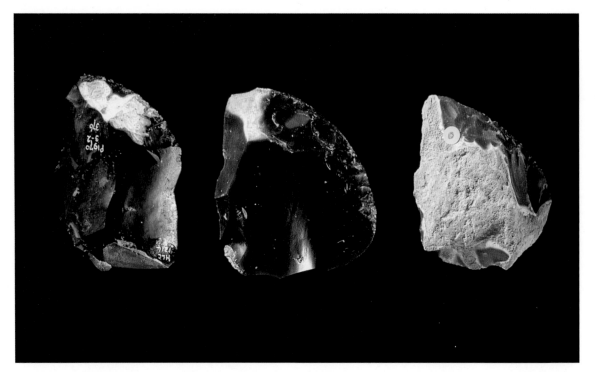

5 Three flake scrapers from the clayey silts at High Lodge (Suffolk). Tools like these were useful for preparing animal hides.

6 Butchery experiment using a handaxe. The handaxe is held between the forefinger and thumb and makes an efficient cutting and skinning tool.

7 Spear II from Schöningen, Lower Saxony, Germany. Project director, Hartmüt Thieme, is seen squatting next to a 2.3m (7.5ft) long spruce wood javelin, which is about 400,000 years old. In the foreground, just to the right of the spear, lies an upturned horse skull.

8 Flat-based Mousterian handaxe (bout coupé) from Bournemouth (Dorset). 2cm scale.

9 Spear-throwing in action. The author dressed to kill on the film set of 'Birth of Europe' launching a spear with an atlatl.

10 Jerzmanovice leaf point from Kent's Cavern (Devon). The broken point is about 10cm (4in) long.

11 Pierced, egg-shaped ivory pendant found in 1912 at Paviland Cave. The pendant fitted a hollow cavity, caused by disease, in a mammoth tusk fragment recovered by Buckland in the 1820s. Shown at about life size.

12 King Arthur's Cave (Herefordshire). The cave was first explored in the 1870s. New excavations by the author between 1995 and 1997 have revealed a long sequence of undisturbed Lateglacial deposits on the right-hand side of the entrance.

13 A Snowy Owl feeding a collared lemming to its young chicks.

14 Collared-lemming limb bones sieved from 'cold deposits' of Loch Lomond Stadial age outside the entrance to King Arthur's Cave.

15 Cheddar points, trapezoidal backed blades, of Late Upper Palaeolithic Creswellian type from Gough's Cave, Cheddar Gorge (Somerset). Longest measures 6cm (2½in).

16 Engraved ivory rod from Pin Hole, Creswell Crags (Derbyshire). The rod is just over 5cm (2in) long.

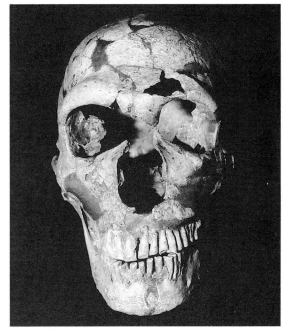

58 Cranium of an adult male Neanderthal from the site of La Ferrassie, south-western France.

57 Reconstruction (1990s) of a Neanderthal in a suit at Erkrath Museum, Germany, based on a modern reassessment of the fossil remains.

Perhaps the most immediately noticeable features of the Neanderthals are in the particular characteristics of the face and head (**58** and **59**). These show a low swept-back forehead with thick brow-ridges and a projecting face with a broad nose. The jutting faces would have been emphasized by the cheek bones angled to the side rather than facing forward as in present-day Europeans. Neanderthals also lacked the strong chins seen in modern people. The skull-shape would have been noticeably different in other respects too, in particular in relation to the back of the head which showed a distinctive bulge known as a 'chignon' or 'occipital bun' with a small dent or *fossa* (**59**). This contributed both in relative and absolute terms to the larger brain volume of

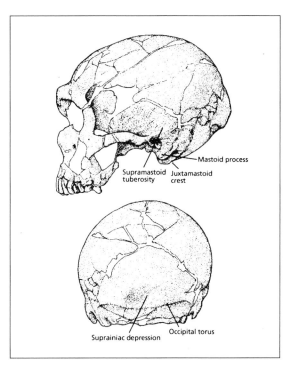

59 Some unique characteristics of the Neanderthal skull.

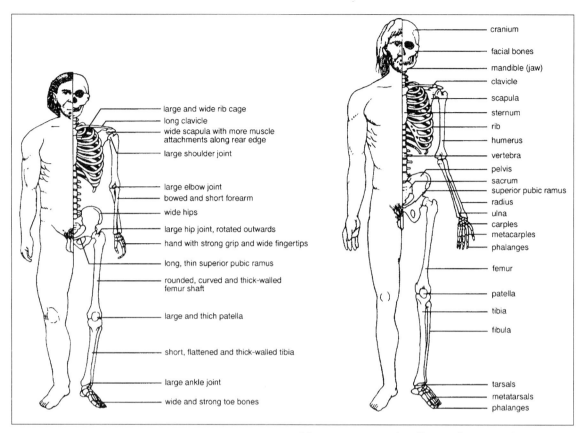

60 Skeleton of a typical male Neanderthal (left) compared with that of a modern male.

Neanderthals compared with the average modern human. While this extra brain space seemingly did not give them greater intelligence, Chris Stringer has noted that the enlarged occipital region coincides with regions of the brain linked with the visual cortex. Although the exact meaning is still unclear, it could imply that Neanderthals had enhanced visual capabilities, perhaps even allowing them to see better in the dark.

Turning to the post-cranial skeleton, Neanderthals possessed markedly different body proportions to modern humans. For example, they had massive barrel-shaped chests with extremely stout bones and powerful musculature (**60**). Their forearms and lower legs were also measurably shorter in relation to the upper parts of the limbs. These features gave them a stocky, thick-set appearance rather

like some arctic dwellers today. Based on modern comparisons such as these, it seems likely that the Neanderthal's physique was 'cold adapted'. The underlying principle behind this interpretation is that a thick, rounded body allows maximum retention of body heat by minimizing the surface area from which heat could be lost. Thus the stocky body-shape of the Neanderthals would have been ideally suited to living in cold climatic conditions. The broad shape of the nose may also have contributed to this adaptation by regulating the temperature of inhaled cold, dry air before it entered the lungs. However, Chris Stringer has rightly drawn attention to the dissimilarities between the nasal openings of Neanderthals and modern peoples living in arctic environments. An alternative theory is that the broad nasal chamber may indeed have acted as an efficient heat exchanger – but for cooling down quickly – after massive exertions in chasing or hunting. A highly ingenious suggestion, also put forward recently, is that a large nose was in fact a focus of sexual attraction. In other words, Neanderthals deliberately chose mates for their impressive conks. In combination with environmental factors, this gave big-nosed individuals selective advantages over their nasally-challenged peers.

Other physical attributes of the Neanderthals may have been less to do with climatic adaptations than the demands of a highly rigorous lifestyle. One of the more interesting areas of recent research concerns the size and thickness of Neanderthal bones. According to the anthropologist Erik Trinkaus the powerful muscle attachments seen in the shoulder and arm implies far greater joint loading capabilities than is found in modern humans. The muscle attachments at the back of the shoulder suggest that Neanderthals were able to exert considerable force in downward throwing and thrusting motions. The anatomy of the hand also shows a much stronger power grip and wider fingertips. This robustness of physique is not only limited to the upper limbs and torso; the lower limbs display an equal strength in the thickness of the bones and joints and in the wide, strong toes. Many of these features are interpreted as adaptations to high levels of prolonged strain. Experimental work into the thickness of bones by the American anthropologist Daniel Lieberman has shown that in animals such as armadillos it is possible to generate extra thick walls on bone artificially by subjecting these animals to greater exercise. If the same idea is applied to the human body, he believes that Neanderthals may have evolved thicker bones in order to deal with habitually greater levels of physical activity. To explain this Lieberman speculates that Neanderthals had to work harder and hunt more actively because they used their environment differently to modern humans.

Another feature apparently unique to the Neanderthals lies in the appearance of the teeth. The front teeth are very large and shovel-shaped, and often show remarkably heavy wear (see **58**). From the degree of rounding and damage present, even sometimes on the teeth of young Neanderthal individuals, it is popularly supposed that the powerful jaws served as a vice or clamp for holding items, rather like an extra hand. Interpretations suggest the wear patterns might be consistent with objects being pulled outwards through tightly clenched teeth. One possibility therefore is that the teeth were used to grip and knead tough objects like animal hides to make them more supple. Equally, from minute scratches on the incisors of Neanderthals, it is possible to infer that meat and other food was held and cut close to the mouth while it was still being eaten. Similar scratches have been noted on the teeth of Inuit who regularly slice meat in this way (**61**).

61 Inuit woman cutting and eating meat with a traditional *ulu* (knife) held close to the mouth.

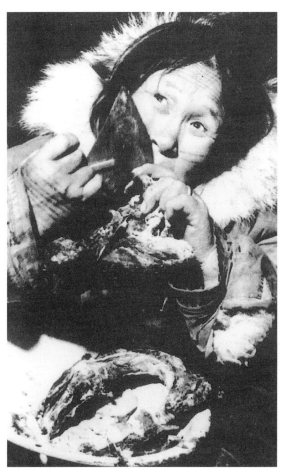

Finally, dental characteristics can provide important evidence of the age of individuals, and have been used to show probable differences in the growth rates of young Neanderthals. For example, analysis of cranial bones of a juvenile Neanderthal from the Devil's Tower, Gibraltar, indicate the child's brain was the same size of a modern four-year-old; yet according to the annual growth rings of the teeth, the child appeared at least a year younger. If both sets of data are correct, then one way of explaining the discrepancy is if Neanderthal children were advanced for their age, or in other words if they grew up faster than modern children. And as Chris Stringer has pointed out, this might have much wider implications for the longer-term survival of the species. A much shorter period of parental care in infancy could have meant less time for learning skills such as language or imparting other knowledge vitally necessary for survival. This could have placed them at a disadvantage to modern humans, and contributed to their extinction, as we shall consider in the following chapters.

Developed language or toddler speak?

While it is not known exactly whether Neanderthals had a sophisticated spoken language like our own, it seems fairly certain that they were able to communicate verbally. For, although none of the soft tissues associated with the voice box or vocal tract are preserved, other fossilized bony structures of the skeleton do indicate that this capacity existed even in very early hominids.

Apart from the large Neanderthal brain, one of the most important pieces of evidence for speech comes from a tiny bone – the hyoid – which lies in the neck and anchors throat muscles necessary for speaking. The fact that a completely modern-looking hyoid was recovered from a 60,000-year-old skeleton from Kebara Cave (Israel), indicates that they may have had modern speech patterns. Against this, however, is the view put forward by Philip Lieberman who reconstructed the vocal tract of the La Chapelle individual. According to his work, the shape of the base of the skull indicates that the voice box must have been located high up in the throat. A similar situation exists in modern infants, where the high voice box only allows a limited range of vocal sounds to be made (but has the adaptive advantage of allowing babies to breath and suckle simultaneously without risk of choking). As the infant grows up so the voice box gradually descends and this in turn is reflected in changes to the underside of the skull which becomes more angular. The relatively flat shape of the La Chapelle basicranium led to the speculation that Neanderthals' speech patterns were infant-like in lacking certain vowel sounds (a, i, u) and consonants (k and g). These ideas, however, have been strongly challenged by the anthropologist Jeff Laitman who has pointed out discrepancies in the original reconstruction of the La Chapelle skull. Using a more accurate reconstruction Laitman has been able to show that the base of the skull was, in fact, strongly angulated as in modern adults.

Thus, it seems that all the necessary vocal apparatus for speech was already present in Neanderthals. But for many specialists this does not prove the argument. For them, the essential key to language lies in the development of suitable brain structures, and, of course, these soft tissues are not preserved in the fossil record. To address such questions one needs to turn instead to the archaeological evidence for clues. But here again the record is disappointingly mute in the case of Neanderthals. Missing in particular, are many of the unmistakable signs of complex symbolic behaviour that we associate with modern humans, and, by extension, with the use of developed language (e.g. wall art, engraved icons, prolific use of red ochre, jewellery). As we shall see in the following chapters, a major change of this type occurs in Europe around 40,000 bp, and it is therefore tempting to place the origins of language at that point. Nevertheless, to take a positive view of Neanderthal abilities, there is every reason to suppose that they had relatively

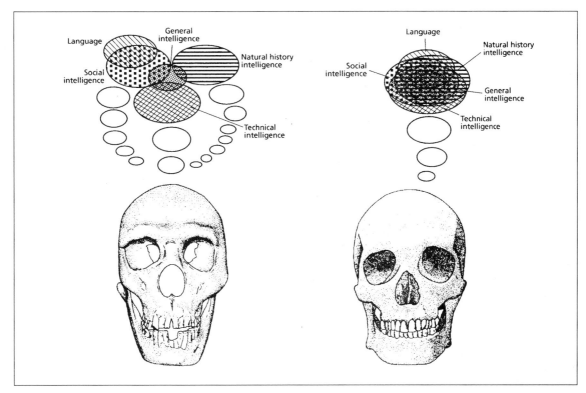

sophisticated communication techniques (whether spoken, or by gesturing or signing); but, to reverse the well-known phrase, it is not how it was said, but what was said that is important. And, for Neanderthals, the scope may have been strictly limited (**62**).

The origins of Neanderthals

The distribution of Neanderthal fossil occurrences covers a wide area of Europe stretching from Gibraltar in the south-west, to Britain and Germany in the north, and extending eastwards as far as Central Asia. There is as yet no Neanderthal evidence from Africa or the Far East.

How Neanderthals evolved characteristics that made them different from other humans is currently not fully understood. One theory put forward by the anthropologist Robert Foley applies to living primates, but may be equally relevant to Neanderthals. According to this idea, if an organism's natural habitat is disrupted, it may lead to a sub-group splitting from the main parent population and becoming geographically

62 The Neanderthal *vs.* the modern human mind. In archaic hominids and Neanderthals language may have been used for processing only certain kinds of information. In modern humans, greater fluidity between the different domains of the brain theoretically allowed a 'general purpose language' to emerge.

isolated. Over a period of time both groups will continue to develop and evolve independently, so that when the habitats are again re-united interbreeding between them is no longer possible. This is exactly what scientists think happened to the chimpanzee, which today forms distinct species, e.g. *Pan troglodytes* (in central east Africa) and *Pan paniscus* (in west Africa). The reasons for the split are not known for certain but it appears likely that part of the ancestral chimpanzee population became geographically isolated, due possibly to changes in the flow of the River Congo. Though there are few physical differences between the two species, they nevertheless do not appear to mate when brought together. Using a broadly similar analogy, it could be hypothesized that the archaic human populations of Europe became an isolated sub-group, possibly due to climatic factors, so that when the geographic ranges again overlapped, several hundred thousand years later, biological and/or behavioural differences were sufficient to prevent successful interbreeding between Neanderthals and anatomically modern humans. This model presupposes that Neanderthals do not belong to the same lineage as modern humans, a subject which is dealt with in more detail in Chapter 7.

Whatever the evolutionary relationships between moderns and Neanderthals, it is widely believed that Neanderthals evolved in Europe or western Eurasia from local populations of *Homo heidelbergensis*, the direct descendants of *Homo erectus* groups that first expanded into western Asia, perhaps 1.8 million years ago (see Chapter 3). Over time these populations gradually evolved morphological characteristics which can be attributed specifically to the Neanderthals.

Pre-Neanderthals

Setting aside current uncertainties about ancestral links, it is clear that there are early fossils which share Neanderthal features. Among this group is the famous Swanscombe skull from the Barnfield Pit in Kent, discovered as three separate fragments in 1935, 1936 and 1955 (**63** and **64**). The cranial pieces fit together perfectly and show characteristics of a modern-looking and relatively large-brained individual (1300ml). A particularly diagnostic feature is a small depression at the back of the skull, known as the suprainiac fossa, which occurs in Neanderthals generally (see **59**), but not in modern humans. Although the skull is often referred to as 'Swanscombe Man', the cranial proportions suggest that of a woman. Unfortunately, due to the skull's incompleteness, it is not possible to be sure what the front of the cranium looked like. But, judging from more complete, contemporary fossils, like that of Steinheim (**64**), it seems probable that she had a

very similar projecting face with angled cheekbones and strong brow ridges, characteristic of Neanderthals.

The dating of the Swanscombe fossil is still a matter of some debate. On geological grounds, it is believed that the Middle Gravels sediments, which yielded the skull, were laid down immediately after the Anglian cold stage (see **Table 2**) when the Thames diverted into its present course. Current opinion therefore favours a warm stage OIS 11 date of about 400,000 years ago for the Swanscombe fossil, although others would see a break in the stratigraphic sequence allowing a somewhat younger (OIS 9) age. If the earlier dating of Swanscombe is right, one of the intriguing issues raised by the fossil, is that it appears more modern-looking than other fossils that could be contemporary or of slightly younger age. One such example is that of Bilzingsleben (Germany), where the fragments of two to three individuals have been found in well-stratified travertine deposits. The fossils reveal a strongly angled back of the head with a developed bony ridge, and together with the small teeth, invite comparisons with those of the ancestral group

63 Pre-Neanderthal cranium from Barnfield Pit, Swanscombe (Kent). The partial skull of a female who lived in Britain about 400,000 years ago.

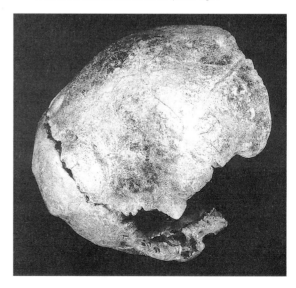

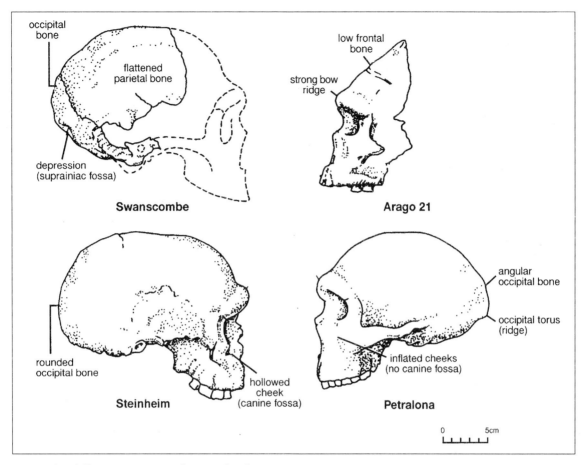

64 European pre-Neanderthals (cf *Homo heidelbergensis*). The reconstruction of the Swanscombe specimen's face is based on that of the Steinheim fossil.

Homo heidelbergensis. According to the dating evidence, the Bilzingsleben fossils can be attributed either to OIS 11 or 9 and therefore are of potentially the same age as Swanscombe or younger. Although the issue over the dating needs to be properly resolved, Chris Stringer suggests that in terms of its evolutionary position the Swanscombe individual probably lies at one end of a spectrum of a single evolving lineage in which the majority of features are Neanderthal-like. Unless there is a great deal of variation in European fossils of this age, this leaves open the possibility of different co-existing hominid species (Swanscombe and Bilzingsleben) living in Europe around 400,000 years ago.

Other fossils of Pre-Neanderthals are known to date from about 200,000 years ago (OIS 7). These include specimens from Ehringsdorf (Germany), Biache (France), and possibly of this age also, Altamura (Italy). In Britain, fossil finds have been recovered from Pontnewydd Cave (north Wales) dating to around 210,000 years ago. Among the remains were twenty human teeth, which show evidence of the clear taurodontism (an enlarged pulp cavity) characteristic of Neanderthals (**65**).

Classic Neanderthals

As mentioned above, the most well-developed Neanderthal characteristics appear in populations living in Europe and western Asia in the period 130,000–30,000 years ago. For this reason individual fossils within this timespan are generally ascribed to the 'classic'

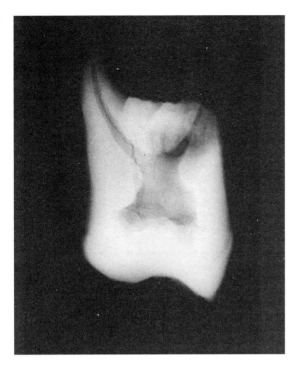

65 Radiograph section through a Neanderthal molar tooth from Pontnewydd Cave showing characteristics of taurodontism (an enlarged pulp cavity). The roots are pointing upwards, the pulp cavity is visible as a dark grey area within the tooth.

Neanderthals and they include the original type fossil from Feldhofer Cave, Neanderthal in Germany.

On the basis of stratigraphical position and the interpretation of associated faunal and floral remains, most of the few hundred Neanderthal fossils from Europe can be dated to the earlier part of the last glaciation – 75,000–30,000 years ago (OIS 3 and 4) – when temperatures dropped on average by about 10°C and the climate was considerably drier (see Chapter 2). However, there is also evidence to show that Neanderthals were present in southern Europe during the preceding interglacial/cool temperate phases 130,000–75,000 years ago (OIS 5a–e), though it is not known whether this involved all or only some of the successive climatic phases. The comparatively rare European fossils of this age probably include those from Saccopastore (Italy) and Krapina (Croatia).

Britain: a Neanderthal desert?

The fact that there is no human fossil evidence in Britain dating from the last interglacial/glacial cycle does not mean that Neanderthals never ranged this far north. Artefacts and occupational debris recorded in cave sites and open locations (see Chapter 6) indicates quite clearly that Neanderthal activities certainly extended well into southern and midland Britain in the last glaciation. Yet it remains true that, in comparison to the density of findspots in mainland Europe, the British record is comparatively sparse and this may reflect the fact that Neanderthals were operating near the extreme northern edge of their range.

Information on the precise timing of Neanderthal activities in Britain is unfortunately still very limited and based largely on typological parallels between British and Continental artefact sequences. In trying to resolve these problems, archaeologist Roger Jacobi and mammal specialist Andrew Currant have turned instead to the fossil mammal record for this period in search of clues for human activities. Their work has concentrated on the re-examination of bone collections for artefact cut-marks or other signs of human modification. By combining this approach with a fresh evaluation of the fossil record, they have been able to argue very convincingly that the appearance of Neanderthals in Britain was probably restricted to the second half of the last glaciation, after about 60,000 years ago (during OIS 3).

The evidence is based on a revised understanding of the chronology of large mammal faunas for the last interglacial/glacial cycle. According to their analyses, no human activity, identified by bone cut-marks or other modification, can be demonstrated on the so-called Hippopotamus faunas of OIS 5e (see Chapter 2). This is perhaps not entirely surprising given the fact that it was one of the few periods in the last 1.8 million years when Britain was completely cut off from the European mainland by high sea-levels. But in addition to the warmest phase, their re-evaluation would suggest that human activities were also absent for a considerable time afterwards (OIS 5a–d and 4) when Britain was again linked to the mainland. Faunal collections for the early part of the glacial (OIS 4) seem to be particularly well represented in British caves. According to Currant and Jacobi they are characterized by a dominance of reindeer and bison (so-called *Banwell*-type faunas after Banwell Bone Cave in Somerset) (see **26**) but none of them has yet produced an association with stone artefacts.

For Currant and Jacobi, the first unequivocal signs of human activity in the last glacial seem to coincide with the arrival of very distinct animals of the 'mammoth steppe'. In Britain these have been named *Coygan*-type faunas after the cave in south-west Wales in which they were recognized (see **27**). Among the animals consistently represented are mammoth, woolly rhinoceros, wild horse and spotted hyena, as well as bear and wolf. Their appearance in Britain seems to be marked by a phase of dry continental climate, in which an open vegetation of mainly grassland extended across much of Europe as far east as Siberia. Although there are as yet few reliable dates it is believed that the period of drier climate began around 60,000 years ago and can be broadly correlated with OIS 3 of the marine record. The fact that stone implements such as Mousterian handaxes have been found with these faunal assemblages suggests that Neanderthals were literally following the animal herds across the open steppe into Britain. In the following chapter we shall examine the evidence for human occupation and the routine lifestyles of Neanderthals in greater detail.

In summary, therefore, it appears that Britain remained largely uninhabited for much of the last interglacial/glacial cycle. This human isolation was probably only broken when foraging and feeding conditions improved to attract populations back into the country. Britain was therefore not a Neanderthal desert, but the arrival of Neanderthals from the Continent was almost certainly delayed until the second half of the last glaciation, after about 60,000 years ago.

6
A highly successful way of life

Ever since the first Neanderthal fossils were discovered in the nineteenth century in Europe, the popular picture of these prehistoric humans has been one of brutish cave-dwellers, relegated to the margins of humanity as an evolutionary sideshow. But in recent years, this image has been transformed by new excavations and analysis which show Neanderthals as fellow human beings with sophisticated tool-making skills and a complex social organization. We know, for example, that they were the first Europeans to bury their dead and, among other advanced behaviours, had developed the potential for speech. Although there is some continuing controversy over the contribution they made to our own evolutionary story, it is now clear they were not the social and intellectual inferiors often portrayed in the past. Far from 'dumb brutes', the Neanderthals were in fact highly intelligent and resourceful creatures, who had overcome most natural obstacles, and became the human survival experts *par excellence* of the Ice Age world.

But how have the ideas on Neanderthals been so radically re-shaped in recent years? What has led us to embrace them again as fellow human beings and how convincing is the evidence on which this reassessment is based?

The framework for re-interpretation

Stone artefacts are the most durable residues of Neanderthal activity. From the analysis of their occurrence at sites, sourcing of lithic raw materials and functional studies of tool-use it is possible to gain a much clearer picture of how Neanderthal activities were organized in the landscape. The implications of such studies are important because they show, among other things, that Neanderthals were capable of overcoming complicated problems and devising flexible solutions, traits of human behaviour often denied them by their critics in the past.

A necessary starting point for analyzing Neanderthal behaviours is an understanding of their Middle Palaeolithic material culture and other traces of activity. Stone artefacts made by Neanderthals have been known and studied for over 150 years. Middle Palaeolithic industries are usually grouped under the name Mousterian, after the site of Le Moustier in the Dordogne in south-west France where excavations were begun by Edouard Lartet in 1863. Following the French discoveries, similar lithic residues (as well as Neanderthal remains) have been uncovered over a very large part of Eurasia from Britain in the west to Uzbekistan in the east. However, while it is useful for working purposes to equate Neanderthals with the Mousterian, the picture is in reality far from simple. For example, some of the earliest European Mousterian industries – at Mesvin in Belgium around 250,000 years ago – were probably made by people ancestral to Neanderthals. Similarly, according to discoveries in the Near East, Mousterian-type artefacts have been found with both

Neanderthal and anatomically modern human fossils. Thus it is important to stress that the Mousterian is only one type of Middle Palaeolithic (or mode 3) industry, albeit one that was used almost exclusively by Neanderthals and their ancestors in Britain and western Europe.

Stone tools and function

Typically, the Mousterian industry is based on the production of flakes, either used simply as sharp cutting edges, or modified into retouched tools. The flake tools generally conform to a restricted range of types which include small triangular points, side-scrapers, notches, denticulates (saw-edge tools), and occasionally thin, flat-based handaxes (**colour plate 8** and see **10**). Such tools are of a highly standardized form and remained essentially unchanged over 100,000 years. Among the distinguishing features of these industries is the use of the Levallois technique, a method of making stone flakes of pre-determined size and thickness (see **9**).

Studies of the function of Mousterian stone tools have relied on shape-edge analysis and experimental replication as well as scientific work on minute polishes (microwear patterns) resulting from tool use. Based on the different frequencies in which tools occur at Mousterian sites, it appears that many of the tool kits were used for processing and maintenance tasks. Tools such as backed knives, notches, denticulates and scrapers were employed in butchery, skinning, scraping and in making other tools out of softer organic materials such as wood. Direct evidence that tools were used in this way comes from wear patterns on the edges of tools which show that hide-scraping and woodworking (chopping and whittling) regularly took place at Mousterian sites. An unexpected source of information on this usage comes from the Romani Rockshelter near Barcelona (north-east Spain), where recent discoveries have revealed the presence of perishable wooden objects normally too fragile to survive in the archaeological record. The

items include a number of flat, elliptical pieces of wood abandoned around a hearth. The objects are slightly dished in the middle leaving the excavators in no doubt that they were platters of some kind, perhaps for holding or processing food. Interestingly, the wood has been identified as juniper, a coarse-grained wood, which is relatively fire-resistant and less prone to warping – thus making it ideal for hearth work. According to the stone tools found, the wooden items were probably made at the site and then deliberately left behind perhaps in anticipation of some future use. Although the Romani platters are so far unique, the manufacture of other wooden objects (such as the spears mentioned in Chapter 4), is well attested earlier in the European record.

Not so well documented, however, are stone tools specifically made for *extractive* tasks such as hunting or plant-harvesting. Indeed, the archaeologist Lewis Binford has for a long time argued that projectile equipment (spears and darts) did not form part of Neanderthal tool kits. Such a view has, however, been increasingly challenged by microwear studies which have shown *hafting* traces at the bases of small triangular stone points indicating how they had been wedged into spearshafts. Traces of bitumen glue have now also been found on Middle Palaeolithic tools from several sites in the Near East – this glue may have been used to secure tool handles. Finally, it should be recalled that if much of the extractive equipment was made of organic material such as wood, these would only survive in exceptional circumstances.

British Mousterian sites

Tools made on Levallois products are known from a number of pre-Neanderthal British sites associated with industries of mode 2 (Acheulian) type. They include Pontnewydd Cave (north Wales) where excavations by Stephen Aldhouse-Green uncovered substantial numbers of scrapers, small handaxes and other flake tools made of local poor quality volcanic rocks (**66**). Other sites

66 Pontnewydd Cave (north Wales). A late Acheulian industry which also contains Levallois artefacts. Amygdaloid (almond-shape) handaxes of local hard rocks including rhyolite (top left) and silicic tuff (bottom right).

of contemporary age (OIS 7), dating to around 200,000 years ago, are characterized by diverse industries, some of which have been termed pre-Mousterian. They include material from La Cotte de St Brelade (Jersey), West Thurrock (Essex) and Bakers Hole, Northfleet (Kent) all of which show a significant use of the Levallois technique. An interesting exception is the site of Stoneham Pit, Crayford (Kent) where an industry based on blade-like flakes was excavated by F. J. C. Spurrell in the 1880s. This fascinating assemblage contains some flakes that can be described as Levallois, but overall the industry reflects a highly flexible approach to the exploitation of good quality flint material and has led some people wrongly to compare it with technologies of Upper Palaeolithic or mode 4 type (see Chapter 1).

On present evidence, the majority of British Mousterian industries probably date to the last

cold stage (60,000–30,000 years ago) and can thus be linked to the activities of classic Neanderthals. The dating is based mainly on the association of Mousterian artefacts with the bones of animals of mammoth-steppe type. As discussed in the previous chapter these are classified as *Coygan* faunas, after the Welsh cave site where uranium series and radiocarbon ages of around 39,000 bp have been obtained on bone specimens.

Following Bordes' classification (see **Table 1**), by far the most common sites in Britain are those of Mousterian of Acheulian Tradition type (MAT), recognizable by the presence of flat-based, cordate handaxes and waste products of their manufacture. A recent survey of these handaxe forms has shown that they are quite widely distributed in caves and open-air findspots across southern, central Midland and western Britain (**67**). Among the best-known examples are those from Oldbury (Kent), Little Paxton (Huntingdonshire), Great Pan Farm, Shide (Isle of Wight), Uphill Cave 8 and Hyaena Den (both in Somerset), Kent's Cavern (Devon) and Coygan Cave (Carmarthenshire). Others have few diagnostic tools but can probably be classified within the same variant because of the presence of handaxe sharpening flakes. A typical case is that of Pin Hole, Creswell Crags (Derbyshire), where axe sharpening flakes have been found together with more primitive-looking choppers and chopping tools. In the opinion of archaeologist Roger Jacobi, this unlikely combination of artefacts is due to the selective use of different raw materials by Neanderthals. The axe flakes are made of a non-local flint and Jacobi has reasonably surmised that these belonged to tools imported to the site. The existence of so few flakes indicates that after use the handaxes were carried away from the site. In contrast, the choppers were of a more intractable local Bunter Quartzite and these were made for immediate purposes only. It is clear therefore that the quality of raw material exerted a considerable influence on the shape of artefacts. It is also worth stressing, as we shall see below, that Neanderthals were capable of relatively sophisticated anticipatory behaviour – in this case by importing flint tools to supplement poorer quality local quartzites. Similar situational responses have been noted at Coygan Cave and Ash Tree Cave (near Creswell) where flat-based handaxes and bifacial axe-thinning flakes of non-local rocks have been found, respectively.

Economic practices: hunting

It was originally proposed by Binford and others that Neanderthals obtained food mainly by foraging and occasional hunting. In other words, they were not hunters in any true sense but obtained plantfoods and meat opportunistically though a mixture of gathering and scavenging, exploiting resources as they were encountered in the landscape. The arguments are for the most part based on animal bone studies and on the absence of 'structure' in the archaeological record. The latter is in fact quite complex to define, but in general it refers to the distribution of artefacts and other materials and the spatial organization of activities within sites. In both cases the patterning contrasts markedly with recorded behaviours of anatomically modern humans.

To begin with, however, let us consider the evidence for organized hunting. In Chapter 4, attention was drawn to finds of wooden throwing spears in association with horse bones at Schöningen (see **colour plate 7**), which date to about 400,000 years ago. While these are undoubtedly from pre-Neanderthal contexts, the site of Lehringen, also in Germany, has produced a pointed piece of yew wood dating to the last interglacial (OIS 5e). It is therefore very likely to have been of Neanderthal manufacture and, given its conspicuous association beneath an elephant carcass, was almost certainly a hunting spear.

Indirect evidence for hunting also comes from various Neanderthal sites where bone remains show that animals were culled, or at least selected, on the basis of age and species. At the

large open-air site at Biache (northern France), for example, the age-mortality profiles of wild cattle indicate that the animals were not the result of windfall scavenging as they included remains of prime adults and not just the weaker individuals. In other instances, at a number of upland sites in the Russian Caucasus, wild goats and sheep appear to have been preferentially culled according to age and at Combe Grenal (south-western France) the age profiles of horse remains do not conform to the patterns which would be expected from simple scavenging. A slightly different situation seems to have existed at Mauran and Le Roc (south-western France) where virtually all of the recovered faunal remains were of large bovids. Butchery marks and the representation of body parts shows that Neanderthals had primary access to all the main

67 Distribution map of flat-based Mousterian handaxes. Site names: 1 Kent's Cavern, 2 Uphill Cave 8, 3 Hyaena Den, 4 Coygan Cave, 5 Great Pan Farm, 6 Little Paxton, 7 Oldbury, 8 Pin Hole, 9 Ashtree Cave.

meat-bearing bones, and this would have been much less likely had the carcasses been scavenged.

The actual methods of hunting are extremely difficult to ascertain. According to several lines of evidence, Neanderthals employed 'confrontational' tactics in which they ran down their prey or attacked them at close quarters. This can be inferred partly from the powerful physique of Neanderthals – the robustness of their bones, for example, suggests that they were capable of producing short bursts of intense physical energy, as in sprinting. Healed injuries found on the bones of Neanderthals also indicate that they regularly survived lacerating body wounds, particularly in the region of the head, neck and upper torso. Until recently, such injuries remained an enigma, but new work by Erik Trinkaus and others has shown some interesting parallels with injuries suffered by modern rodeo riders. It would suggest that the throwing spears were not always effective weapons, since the animals had to be approached very closely in order to be killed.

One of the most dramatic examples of Neanderthal hunting strategy comes from La Cotte de St Brelade (Jersey), which dates back to the penultimate cold stage (OIS 6). The site is situated at the foot of a 30m-deep (100ft) ravine at the end of a windswept headland, and served as a pitfall trap for twenty mammoths (adults and young) and five woolly rhinos. How people managed to drive the animals to their deaths remains a mystery, but it is likely to have required the cooperation of many individuals. There is also evidence that this happened on two separate occasions as revealed by bone heaps in two stratigraphic levels, each with many associated stone artefacts. The absence of carnivore damage on the bones and the observation that the mammoth skulls were deliberately smashed open (perhaps for the extraction of brain tissue) again seem to rule out secondary scavenging by humans.

The recognition of structured hunting practices in the archaeological record, no matter how slight, is important because it marks a significant threshold in the evolution of advanced human behaviour. Among other things it implies organizational abilities and the capacity to think and plan ahead. Weighing up the evidence at our disposal it seems highly likely that Neanderthals regularly obtained meat by hunting.

Other foraging activities

While it is important to stress the potential of hunting as the main source of meat in the Neanderthal diet, its overall significance should not be exaggerated. It is clear, for example, that scavenging provided a viable alternative, and may sometimes have been used instead of hunting, as the situation demanded.

Researchers Mary Stiner and Steven Kuhn have demonstrated that for Neanderthal sites on the west coast of Italy, scavenging activities were particularly prevalent in this area after the last interglacial (from about 120,000 years ago). According to them scavenging is signalled by the presence of cranial remains and marrow bones which were collected either from natural casualties or animals killed by other carnivores. But, at a later date, after 50,000 years ago, hunting became more common, as shown by whole carcasses of red deer and fallow deer caught and brought back to sites for butchery.

In some ways the arguments about hunting vs. scavenging have tended to overshadow the part played by plant foods in archaic diets. This is, of course, mainly due to the fact that fragile botanical remains rarely survive in the archaeological record. Nevertheless it should be remembered that in most environments fruits and root vegetables contribute significantly to overall human food consumption. In some recorded instances plantfoods can be shown to make up around 70 per cent of the hunter-gatherer diet. A similar situation may have existed for Neanderthals, although the vagaries of preservation mean that we only rarely have glimpses of the types of plantfoods eaten.

A rare example of this kind comes from Gorham's Cave (Gibraltar) where Mousterian levels reveal small hearths and a range of carbonized plant residues including wild olive seeds and stone-pine nuts. The presence of large natural stones in the same levels suggest that these foods were being processed and eaten at the site (**68**). A similar situation has been recorded in Israel at Kebara Cave where it appears that wild peas were parched in hearths that were also being used for general cooking purposes. Quite independently, Lewis Binford has proposed a possible correlation between the frequency of notched and denticulated stone tools at sites and woodworking practices or the preparation of plant foods. Such models will need to be tested against other evidence (e.g. microwear analysis) but it does suggest a promising avenue for future research. In addition to plantfoods, the contribution of other harvested foodstuffs should not be forgotten.

68 Large rounded 'grinding' stones associated with carbonized plant remains in one of the Mousterian levels from Gorham's Cave, Gibraltar.

For example, a range of edible shellfish and small reptiles, like land tortoises, are known from various coastal Mediterranean sites. Any or all of these foods were probably regularly consumed because they were reliable and relatively easy to collect.

Use of the landscape

As a rule, it is generally accepted that Neanderthals led a highly nomadic existence, moving many times in the course of the annual cycle. In itself this does not inform our ideas about their behaviour since it differs little from the behaviour of modern ethnographic hunter-gatherers, like the !Kung San of the Kalahari. A more rewarding approach is to consider *how* they used the landscape and in what ways this differed from modern humans.

The study of raw materials and stone artefacts has thrown significant new light on Neanderthal behaviour, particularly in the realm of understanding mobility patterns and their degree of forward planning. For prehistoric

people largely dependent on a stone technology, there must have been a constant need to replenish supplies of suitable materials for toolmaking. Underpinning this principle is the idea that effort (*costs*) are involved in finding, making and maintaining stone tools. The costs are, however, not constant or evenly incurred, but will vary according to whether workable stone is locally available or whether it has to be imported from distant sources.

Based on ethnographic evidence, the archaeologist Lewis Binford proposed two models of raw material activity that would leave behind distinctive *signatures* in the archaeological record. In the first model, the use of local rock is equated with on-the-spot manufacture of tools and flakes that are then immediately thrown away after use: these are characterized as disposable or *expedient* toolkits. In contrast, the second model predicts that the further a site is from sources of good quality raw materials, the more likely it is that artefacts will have been imported. Applying the economy principle, the lightest way of transporting stone is in the form of finished tools. Moreover, because this incurs costs in terms of effort, the tools would be expected to bear extended signs of use and re-sharpening: in other words, the tools would be more carefully maintained or, in Binford's words, *curated*.

For Binford, such raw material signatures are important because they allow recognition of distinct modes of behaviour, and even levels of ability, that might not be shared equally among all archaic humans. Accordingly, he sees a sharp distinction between fully modern humans and Neanderthals in the ability of moderns to plan and think ahead. This would be signalled in the Upper Palaeolithic record by a greater reliance on curated toolkits (see Chapter 7). If the presumption is correct then, by the same token, we would expect to find far less evidence of transported equipment and more examples of expedient toolkits at Neanderthal sites. In fact, reappraisal of Mousterian lithic assemblages has shown the reverse. It seems

Neanderthals were much more flexible in their raw material acquisition than would otherwise be predicted; they employed a range of strategies as the situation demanded. For example, while there is plentiful evidence of local raw material use at Mousterian sites, very often there is a small but significant admixture of tools – such as handaxes – made of exotic rocks which show signs of curation. In other words, it seems clear that Neanderthals were certainly capable of some forms of anticipatory behaviour and planning for future needs. At La Quina in south-western France there is evidence that recycling and intensive re-sharpening (curation) was *also* undertaken on artefacts made of local raw materials, which would seem to contradict the established model for curated technologies.

Recent work on Mousterian sites in France by the archaeologist Jean-Michel Geneste has tended to confirm the complexity of Neanderthal exploitation of raw materials. He has shown, for example, that traces of Mousterian occupation generally occur in two forms. The first is represented by sites with relatively low densities of artefacts found widely scattered in the landscape. The site scatters consist mainly of unretouched flakes made from locally available raw materials, and occasionally tools such as handaxes. According to Geneste, these are disposable toolkits and probably reflect episodic activities, linked to opportunistic hunting and feeding activities. The second form of occupation evidence, especially common in large caves and rockshelter sites in south-west France, consists of much larger scatters of material, often many layers thick, and probably reflecting repeated use of these places over hundreds or even thousands of years. The range of artefacts can include tools made of local raw materials, as well as implements brought in from distances of up to 100km (62 miles). The imported items are often retouched tools with heavy signs of use and resharpening. Thus, in these instances the evidence points to a mixture of curated and expedient raw material behaviour.

In Britain, Mousterian sites seem to fit the pattern of Geneste's low density artefact scatters that are widely dispersed in the landscape. The open-air sites are predominantly of MAT type containing small quantities of finished tools, such as flat-based handaxes (also referred to as *bout coupé* handaxes) and unretouched flakes. Following Derek Roe's observations, some patterning may be visible in the distribution of open-air findspots which tend to cluster on major river valleys in southern and eastern England. Whether the gaps in between are more apparent than real is still not clear, but it seems likely that Neanderthals were operating in very low numbers in Britain, and that river valleys would have provided the most convenient means of traversing the landscape, as well as providing constant access to water supplies.

Evidence of Neanderthal activity in Britain is not solely restricted to open-air sites; caves and rockshelters were used extensively in western and north-central Britain. According to the small number of assemblages that have been systematically analyzed it appears that frequent, expedient use was made of local raw materials, sometimes with the addition of imported tools made from more distant lithic sources. However, there are exceptions to the rule, such as Hyaena Den (Somerset) where most of the lithic assemblage, which includes handaxes, is made of relatively local chert.

One of the interesting features of the British open-air and cave locations (see **67**) is that the recorded assemblages are essentially very similar. They contain small accumulations of tools and waste and can be interpreted as low density sites, occupied for only short periods. Of course, some variation might be expected in this pattern, particularly in cases where sites were visited on more than one occasion, as has been postulated for Kent's Cavern. According to nineteenth-century excavation records of this cave, William Pengelly recovered over 1,000 stone artefacts from a loamy earth mostly within the Great Chamber of the cave, although it is possible that the finds are a mixture of

MAT and younger material. The site is of particular interest because it also contains a rich *Coygan*-type fauna, dominated by hyena, woolly rhinoceros and wild horse (see **27**). Sadly, relatively little of the total collection is preserved today. The finds include five small sub-triangular and cordiform handaxes and various typical side-scrapers. Even though the site is regarded as 'rich' by British standards, it still conforms to the overall pattern of small sites in a European sense. To reiterate: little distinction can be drawn between Mousterian open-air sites and cave sites in Britain; both seem to reflect similar activities within the context of brief occupations.

The question of mobility in Neanderthal societies remains an intriguing one. According to the raw material data, patterns of behaviour may have varied from region to region. Thus the evidence for western Europe implies relatively sedentary behaviour, with distances seldom exceeding 50km (31 miles), but this contrasts with eastern and central Europe where it is not unusual to find raw materials originating from over 100km (62 miles) away. Britain seems to follow the pattern established for western Europe, with lithics probably moving over short distances, except in exceptional circumstances as at Coygan Cave in south Wales, where the distance was probably closer to 100km. In the case of central Europe the longer distances may simply be due to an incomplete knowledge of raw material distribution and this pattern may therefore change over time.

The idea of mobility has also been explored from a slightly different angle in the Near East. Here, the anthropologist Daniel Lieberman analyzed animal remains from various Neanderthal and modern human cave occupations in Israel. From the study of gazelle teeth he was able to distinguish very different exploitation patterns: the Neanderthals trapped or hunted these animals all year round, but the moderns appear to have culled gazelle seasonally. According to Lieberman, the strategy employed by the Neanderthals was less effective, because it led to local depletion in game resources and gave rise to reduced protein yields from nutritionally poor animals. To overcome these shortcomings, he believes that the Neanderthals had to work much harder in obtaining foods. Although they gained access to gazelle meat all year round they had to travel further and further afield in order to obtain it. This form of behaviour required much greater mobility and meant that Neanderthals probably spent much more time actively engaged in finding food than did modern people in a similar situation.

Site structure and internal organization

Relatively little work has so far been published on how Neanderthals organized and used space at an individual site level. At Combe Grenal cave in south-western France, original living floors have been excavated which reveal distinct patterning in the distribution of bones and stone artefacts. In one area associated with ashy hearth deposits, scatters of splintered marrow bones and smashed cranial material were recovered together with tools made from local raw materials. Nearby, other concentrations consisted of stone tools made from non-local rocks and linked to heavily carbonized hearth deposits. According to Lewis Binford, these two sorts of concentrations represent two very different kinds of economic activity. His explanation is that the small nests of bone and flint were made by females who foraged in the immediate vicinity of the cave for plant materials and scavenged animal parts. The other scatters were generated by males who ranged more widely and who probably ate the best of the hunted meat at the locations where the animals were killed. He believes that the males brought home only the long bones and heads to be splintered for marrow extraction. Whether or not such an interpretation is valid, it nevertheless raises the interesting question: did women and men forage together or did they follow totally separate economic lives? According to the physical evidence of hunting

injuries and tooth-wear patterns, which are fairly evenly divided between males and females, the answer seems to be that there was no obvious division of labour between the sexes.

Activities at the fireside

One of the most vital adaptations in a cold temperate climate must have been the ability to control and create fire. Apart from warmth-giving, fire served a variety of functions. Meat could be defrosted (allowing access to frozen carcasses) or roasted over the open flame to improve its taste and kill parasites. In addition to cooking, fire provided an important light-source and essential protection against predators. In Europe, ample evidence of firemaking has been found at Mousterian sites. Fireplaces or hearths are known from both open-air sites and caves. The existence of these features presupposes an important social role in bringing families and groups together, but nevertheless certain features of Neanderthal hearths imply a more limited function. This is partly due to the simplicity of the structures, which are generally small bowl-shaped scoops, and suggest only very brief use, perhaps overnight. On the other hand, recent discoveries at Gibraltar and other European sites hint at a greater diversity of hearth types than has been supposed. For example at Vanguard Cave (Gibraltar) there are multiple combustion zones (**69**). These are placed close to the cave wall and may indicate repeated use of the same place for roasting meat and cracking bones for marrow.

By analyzing the occupational residues around hearths, some specialists have come to the conclusion that Neanderthals probably did not spend much time socializing at the fireside. Although there is plenty of evidence of waste flakes and bone debris around the ashy patches, it is clear that the processing of carcasses and other subsistence activities often occurred away from the fire. As a result, specialists like Clive Gamble doubt that hearths were places where Neanderthals sat cosily together exchanging ideas and information. He compares the

69 Combustion zone from a Mousterian level at Vanguard Cave, Gibraltar.

evidence with that of Upper Palaeolithic sites (younger than 30,000 years ago) where the hearths are more complex (being lined with stones) and where the surrounding debris is more evenly scattered. According to him, the more structured arrangement in these cases implies greater interaction between individuals. Recent analysis of Mousterian hearths at Grotte XVI in the Dordogne (France) does show that Neanderthals made and deposited artefacts by the light of the fire, but the excavators of the site believe this was the product of short-term activities. Such an interpretation would, of course, conveniently fit Gamble's ideas of only brief opportunities for social exchange, perhaps further inhibited by the absence of language (discussed in Chapter 5). In Britain, the existence of hearths, though rare, is indicated by

burnt bones and artefacts from a number of Mousterian cave sites.

Symbolic and ritual behaviour

There can be little doubt that Neanderthals had developed recognizably modern human attitudes to death. While it is not clear whether they had sophisticated religious or spiritual beliefs, they certainly seem to have developed emotional attachments to individuals with their society. Evidence of this behaviour is found in the existence of deliberate burials and in the sometimes complex treatment received by bodies in the mortuary process.

Burials have been discovered in a number of different cave sites and rockshelters in Eurasia. Burials at open-air sites have been found only rarely, but this is to be expected given the problems of preservation in exposed situations. Sadly, no convincing examples of either kind have yet been found in Britain.

Some of the earliest funerary practices in the world may be linked to pre-Neanderthals living in Europe over 300,000 years ago. One of the earliest claims comes from the Sima de los Heusos, a small chamber deep within Atapuerca Cave (but in a different location to the site mentioned in Chapter 3), where the remains of over thirty human individuals have been recovered. It was originally proposed that the dead had been thrown down the shaft, partly because of the inaccessibility of the chamber and partly because some of the bones were still in articulation. However, this view has recently been strongly challenged by palaeontologist Peter Andrews and others who have made a careful analysis of the human remains. According to their findings, gnaw marks on the bone indicate the work of carnivores, probably lions, who may have dragged human prey into their cave dens.

More convincing forms of burial have been found at later rockshelters and caves in association with classic Neanderthals (**70**). These illustrate that the dead were interred in shallow, hand-dug graves sometimes associated with simple grave goods of bone or flint. The method most frequently used was to place the body on its side, either with the arms and legs tightly flexed (like an unborn child) or with one hand drawn up to the face, suggesting an attitude of sleep or repose. From the tightly constricted attitude of the corpses they may have been tied up with a cord or thong prior to burial. Alternatively, burial could have taken place before *rigor mortis* had fully set in. While we may never know the direct significance of the body settings, it is tempting to interpret the foetal positions and the gestures of sleeping/re-awakening as metaphors for entering and leaving the world.

The grave goods associated with Neanderthal burials are generally very rudimentary, consisting of stone tools and ochre fragments (as at La Chapelle-aux-Saints in France) or animal parts (Roc de Marsal and La Quina in France) or natural stones forming part of the burial

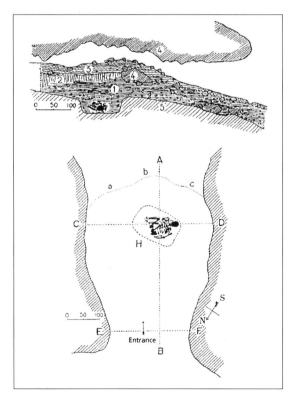

70 Section and plan of the Neanderthal burial at La Chapelle-aux-Saints (south-western France).

structure (Le Moustier, La Ferrassie and Regourdou in France and Shanidar, Iraq). Recent literature on the subject has tended to downplay the importance of Neanderthal burials, comparing them with everyday methods of rubbish disposal rather than special interments. The question has arisen partly because of existing doubts over the context of the finds: some were supposedly found in the middle of domestic refuse, while others were inexpertly recorded in the nineteenth century. In certain quarters, this has led to the wholesale dismissal of Neanderthal burials as being without any great sense of organization or ceremonial purpose.

Such views are almost certainly wrong because they fail to take into account all of the available evidence. One of the most convincing arguments for purposeful burial comes from the rockshelter of La Ferrassie where a small cemetery of pits with two adults and five young Neanderthals appears to have been laid out in a deliberate fashion. Some of the pits were covered by stone cairns, while two of the others were deliberately juxtaposed so that the adult individuals lay head to head. At other sites, such as the cave of Roc de Marsal, the burial pits seem to have been deliberately placed at the boundary between the light and dark zones of the cave. A further objection relates to the implied simplicity of the burial rites themselves. First, the lack of burial goods may in no way reflect the potential richness of the funeral ceremony itself. Indeed, on the criterion of grave goods alone, a modern Christian burial would appear far less sophisticated than a Neanderthal one! Equally, it could be argued that the position or gesture of the buried corpse could convey a sense of meaning every bit as important as any number of accompanying artefacts. The fragility of wood, bark and other plant matter could also mean that only in exceptional circumstances would we be aware of associated grave items. A particular case in point is the famous flower burial from Shanidar Cave (Iraq). The burial of an old man (Shanidar

4) revealed high concentrations of pollen from a wide range of wild flowers, some with medicinal properties. According to the excavator, the body must have been wreathed in flowers, although others have explained the presence of pollen in terms of modern contamination.

Probably the most intriguing aspect of Neanderthal ritual activity, and one that has emerged only recently, is the practice of secondary or two-stage burial involving excarnation. Evidence for this activity comes in the form of deliberate cut-marks on the skulls and body parts of several Neanderthal individuals made after death. According to some specialists, the incisions at the back of the skull, present on the original Neanderthal fossil from Germany and those from Krapina (Croatia) are consistent with cuts made when disarticulating the skulls, presumably so they could be exposed or re-buried elsewhere. Some support for this idea may come from the Kebara fossil from Israel where only the skull is missing, although factors such as natural erosion cannot be entirely ruled out. A more chilling interpretation of these occurrences is that they represent some form of ritual cannibalism. In this view, cut-marks and fractures are seen as indicating ceremonial defleshing, involving scalping and perhaps the consumption of the soft tissues of the brain. Certainly, cut-marks and fresh bone breakage have been recognized on Neanderthal post-cranial remains from Krapina and Vindija (Croatia), Combe Grenal and Abri Moula (France), and these are difficult to explain purely in terms of secondary burial. It is also interesting that some of the modifications appear to be identical with those on animal bones in the same deposits.

Other signs of symbolic behaviour can perhaps be recognized in the few pieces of abstract engraving from Neanderthal sites, such as the fossil pebble with an engraved cross (71) from Tata in Hungary or the marked bone from Combe Grenal, France. Generally, however, these items are extremely rare, and together with the total absence of cave paintings, imply that ritual activities were strictly limited. Claims have also

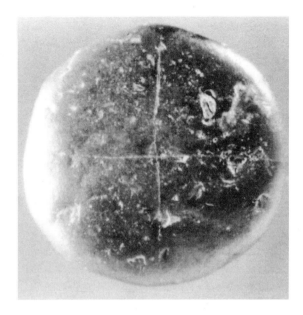

71 Engraved pebble from Mousterian levels at Tata, Hungary. A nummulite fossil on which a line was incised at right angles to a natural crack running through the fossil.

been made for musical instruments (whistles and flutes), but these can nearly always be discounted as pseudofacts. Nevertheless, one of the problems in approaching this question is in recognizing the products of behaviour which may be manifestly unfamiliar to the modern mind. One possible example is a strange four-sided structure discovered recently, deep underground in the cave systems of Bruniquel, south-western France. Based on the dating of associated burnt bone, the rectangular structure – measuring 4m by 5m (12 by 15ft) and made up of fallen slabs of stalagmite – is dated to over 47,600 years. The discoverers are in no doubt that the artificial walling was constructed by Neanderthals, far beneath the ground surface, in a relatively inaccessible place. However, the reason for this isolated structure, possibly a signpost or marker, still remains wholly enigmatic.

Tailpiece

Whether or not Neanderthals engaged in social activities or gossiped around the fireplace, it is impossible not to see them as advanced human beings who lived communally, in relatively large groups. From wear patterns on their front teeth and tiny cut-marks left by flint meat knives, we can assume that, like us, they were predominantly right-handed. Equally, we can be fairly certain they hunted, at least on an opportunistic basis, and that this involved group cooperation. Moreover, Neanderthals were highly proficient craftsmen who possessed considerable technical skills, which they used to good effect in a wide range of different habitats. They controlled fire to generate heat and light, they had a sophisticated knowledge of different raw materials including stone and wood. Above all, probably the most humanizing aspect of their behaviour was that they deliberately buried their dead.

In other respects, however, they were not particularly modern. They did not build complicated hearths and nor is there much evidence that they engaged in making shelters or other structures. Internally, their sites were not formally organized – there is scant evidence of either shared spaces or even special areas for dumped refuse. There are few pits and no indications of any storage facilities. Where it exists, food processing equipment is of a relatively unsophisticated and rudimentary nature. Males and females seem to have led equally physically demanding lives and there is nothing in their healed bone injuries to suggest that hunting or other activities were divided along gender lines. And, of course, they left virtually no art or other lasting evidence of symbolic expression.

In Britain we have plenty of evidence of Neanderthal activities even though their skeletal remains are scarce. Here, at the extreme northern edge of their range, they operated very much as they did elsewhere in Europe. They roamed widely and moved frequently, but, as far as we can tell, always in small numbers. Their arrival in Britain coincided with appearance of mammoth-steppe faunas of *Coygan*-type, so in some respects they were merely another element of the shifting animal community. Nevertheless, in the end, we are left with the impression of a highly gifted people who survived in Europe for a much longer time than we have so far managed. Perhaps rather than considering them as failed models of ourselves, it is high time they were treated as advanced humans in their own right.

7
Anatomically modern humans and the Upper Palaeolithic

One of the most intriguing problems facing archaeologists is how to interpret relatively sudden cultural changes in the archaeological record. A particularly fascinating example concerns the period known as the Middle-Upper Palaeolithic transition. It covers the time between 40,000 and 30,000 bp when Neanderthals became extinct and when the earliest evidence for modern *Homo sapiens sapiens* is found in Europe. Coinciding with this major threshold in human evolution is the appearance of a radically different material culture – the Upper Palaeolithic. The aim of this chapter is to characterize the archaeological record of change and to examine how and when the transition to modern behaviour took place. The question of the transition is particularly relevant in the case of Britain because of the great diversity of archaeological evidence for this period and because of Britain's special geographical position, lying on the extreme edge of the inhabited Palaeolithic world.

All about Eve

The earliest anatomically modern human populations in Europe are known as Cro-Magnons after the rockshelter in south-west France where the first fossil discoveries were made in 1868. Since they share most of our own physical characteristics they are classified within the same species of *Homo sapiens sapiens*. However, even though we occupy the same lineage as Cro-Magnons, the origin of our modern species is still a hotly debated subject.

According to conventional wisdom, the origin of modern *sapiens* lies outside Europe in Africa. Chris Stringer one of the leading proponents of this idea has argued that the common ancestor of all living people evolved in Africa sometime between 200,000 and 100,000 years ago. Following outward dispersal (in much the same way as the first expansion, over a million years earlier, described in Chapter 3) modern people gradually colonized the Old World, replacing existing archaic populations in each of these areas; in Europe, for example, they replaced Neanderthals, as indicated by the dating of fossil finds. Fossil evidence in the Near East at Qafzeh and Skhūl Caves (Israel) identifies the most likely route taken by humans out of Africa. Independently derived genetic evidence also supports the African Exodus model; it suggests we can trace back our collective ancestry, using mitochondrial (mt)DNA transmitted only through the maternal line, to a single woman – named 'African Eve'. Based on estimates of mutation rates of mtDNA, geneticists can place this event at about 150,000 years ago. This is remarkably close to the dates first proposed by Stringer.

Not everyone necessarily agrees with the recent Out of Africa model. An alternative theory put forward by anthropologist Milford Wolpoff and others suggests that modern humanity evolved independently and more or less simultaneously in several different parts of the world. This multiregional theory of human

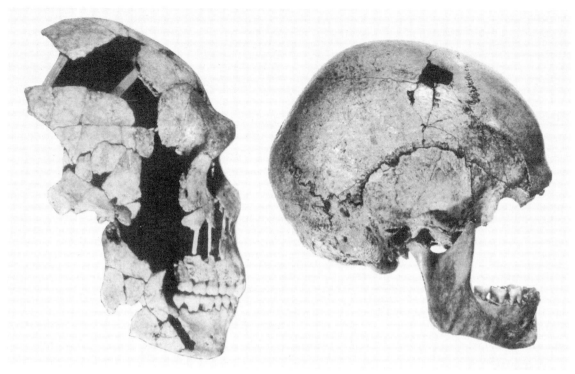

72 Late Neanderthal cranium from the Châtelperronian levels (*c.* 35,000 bp) at Saint-Césaire, south-west France (left); anatomically modern human skull from the early Aurignacian levels at Vogelherd, southern Germany (right).

origins also places our ancestry in Africa but to a hominid living over a million years ago – *Homo erectus*. In Wolpoff's view, there was only one major dispersal of hominids out of Africa. In other words, a direct line of ancestry can be traced in Europe from *Homo erectus* via Neanderthals to modern *Homo sapiens*.

Today, few informed anthropologists accept the multiregionalist argument because it simply does not fit the available evidence, at least in Europe. To begin with, it has become increasingly clear that Neanderthals survived much longer than previously thought. Their archaeological remains have been found in southern Spain as late as 30,000 years ago and, as we will see in this chapter, the earliest European modern humans and their archaeology can be dated to at least 40,000 years ago. This leaves a considerable time

overlap between the two hominids that cannot be explained by evolutionary change alone (**72**). In the Near East too, modern humans and Neanderthals can be shown to have occupied contemporary environments around 90,000 years ago, with Neanderthals surviving in this region until at least 60,000 years ago. Whichever way you look at the evidence, there simply was not enough time for Neanderthals to have evolved into modern humans. The most satisfactory explanation therefore is the one proposed by Stringer and others whereby Neanderthals were replaced by moderns. In Europe, the process seems to have been a very gradual one as implied by almost 10,000 years of coexistence. A further dramatic twist to this debate has come with the announcement of the first successful extraction of ancient DNA from a Neanderthal bone. According to preliminary reports, released as this book goes to press, Neanderthals do not share the same genetic sequences as ourselves, implying that they were a distinct species and thus ruling out any interbreeding with early modern humans, at least in the case of the Neanderthal specimen sampled (the type specimen from the Neander valley). If this is confirmed, it means that the Neanderthals could not possibly have been our direct ancestors and this would disprove the multiregionalist argument once and for all.

Physical appearance of Cro-Magnons

Well-preserved skeletons in caves and rockshelters, like the ones from the Cro-Magnon site itself, provide us with a good idea of what the early moderns looked like. They suggest a people remarkably similar to ourselves, with high, rounded braincases and typically steep foreheads behind small facial brows (73). Their faces were relatively flat and neatly 'tucked in' beneath the cranium, unlike the distinctly jutting face of the Neanderthals. They also had a slightly smaller brain than Neanderthals. For example, Cro-Magnon 1 had an estimated cranial capacity of 1600 ml, as opposed to about 1740 ml for some

Neanderthals. Other features of the head and face were equally distinctive. The back of the head was more rounded and, at the front, the eye orbits were much squarer, emphasizing the small nose and prominent but hollowed cheek bones. Unlike Neanderthals, the chin was accentuated.

The rest of the trunk and body shows that Cro-Magnons were taller and more slenderly built than Neanderthals. This is illustrated particularly in the greater length of the forearms and lower limbs. The shapes of the upper leg and the pelvis reveal that Neanderthals probably had a slightly different walking motion compared with moderns. Age estimates of skeletons suggest that Cro-Magnons were relatively long-lived. Cro-Magnon 1, for

73 Adult male Cro-Magnon (*Homo sapiens sapiens*) from the rockshelter of the same name in Les Eyzies, Vezère, south-west France.

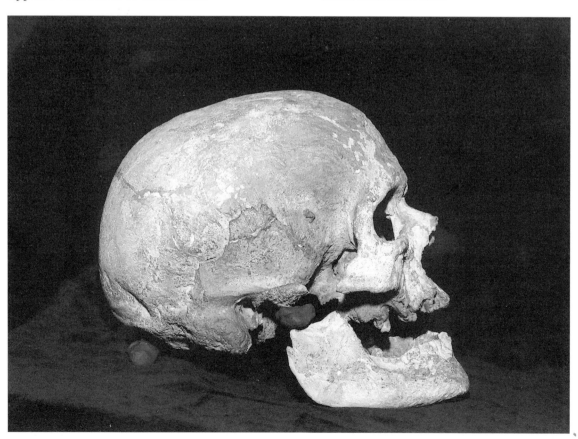

example, was around fifty years old when he died; such an age would be regarded as exceptional for Neanderthals, most of whom had a maximum life expectancy of only about thirty-five years.

The physical proportions of the body hold vital clues about the geographical origins of our species. Using modern comparative evidence it can be shown that people with lanky, cylindrical bodies and long limbs have definite advantages over people with more spherical body shapes in warmer climates. This is because a tall, long-legged physique allows the body's heat to dissipate more easily. The body proportions of the tall Cro-Magnons seem therefore to offer compelling evidence that *Homo sapiens* had evolved in the tropical climates of Africa rather than Europe.

In nearly all respects Cro-Magnons seem totally modern, but there are in fact one or two interesting anomalies. These are revealed particularly in skull shape and dentition which indicate that the early moderns had slightly larger teeth, bigger brains and marginally flatter faces than our own even though the cheekbones were more prominent. Moreover, reconstructions of the rest of the body show they were on average taller than people today but, according to bone density measurements,

probably weighed more or less the same. For Chris Stringer and others, these distinctions are relatively superficial and not significant enough to imply major evolutionary differences. For example the slightly enhanced brain size may simply have been due to a relatively larger body size; indeed some of the skull measurements of Cro-Magnons fall within the variation expected in modern living populations.

Examples of early Cro-Magnon fossils are known in Britain from Kent's Cavern (Devon)(74) and Paviland Cave (West Glamorgan). These will be considered in more detail below.

Upper Palaeolithic: the mother of all inventions

Cro-Magnons are invariably found with a material culture known as Upper Palaeolithic, which marks a distinct break with the traditions of the Middle Palaeolithic. Among the innovative features of this technology were improved methods of working stone and other materials, new forms of stone tools, the manufacture of a wide range of bone, antler and ivory artefacts, and the first appearance of various types of personal ornaments including decorated art forms. Further changes in this period are indicated by significant advances in human organizational abilities which, among other things, gave rise to reliable storage methods, long-distance movement of flint and shells, new hunting techniques and highly elaborate burials. All of these features show a major break in continuity with the preceding Middle Palaeolithic (Mousterian) industries.

Before describing these changes in more detail it is essential to realize that the Upper Palaeolithic revolution was not instantaneous but involved a constant process of experiment and evolution taking many thousands of years. Following the classic French terminology, the Upper Palaeolithic can be divided into a number of cultural sub-stages defined chronologically and on the basis of progressive developments in artefact forms.

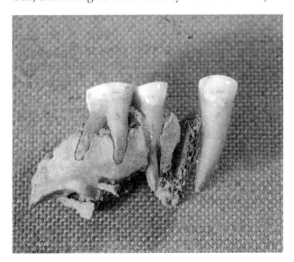

74 Kent's Cavern modern human (*Homo sapiens sapiens*) upper jaw AMS dated to about 31,000 bp.

The Aurignacian, the Upper Perigordian (known as the Gravettian outside France) and the Solutrean can all be identified with the phase of the Early Upper Palaeolithic, preceding the coldest part of the last glaciation (about 18,000 bp). According to present estimates, the Last Glacial Maximum marks a distinctive hiatus in the occupation of northern Europe, during which human activity either ceased altogether or was so intermittent as to be archaeologically invisible. Following climatic improvement after about 15,000 bp, many regions north of the River Loire were recolonized by hunter-gatherers who possessed a distinctive material culture known as the Magdalenian. The Magdalenian, its variants and successors (e.g. Hamburgian, Creswellian, Federmesser, Ahrensburgian) can all be grouped together under the term Late Upper Palaeolithic, a phase that terminates with the onset of postglacial conditions about 10,000 bp.

The oldest Upper Palaeolithic technology in Europe is the Aurignacian, after the French type-site of Aurignac where such finds were first recognized. The earliest dating of the Aurignacian in association with anatomically modern human remains so far comes from Bacho Kiro in Bulgaria. Here the industry is dated to more than 43,000 bp, although some suspect the security of this radiocarbon date. Nevertheless, additional corroboration of the early dating comes from other Aurignacian findspots in eastern Europe, such as Temnata (Bulgaria), Istállóskö (Hungary) and Willendorf (Austria) all of which are believed to be over 40,000 years old. Until recently, rather later dates were recorded for the Aurignacian in western Europe (e.g. 34,000 bp at Abri Pataud, south-west France) and this supported the idea of progressive expansion from east to west. Lately, however, new evidence from several sites in northern Spain has cast doubt on this interpretation. Radiocarbon dates of 38,000–40,000 bp from El Castillo in Cantabria and at one or two other sites in the western Mediterranean imply a simultaneous appearance of the Aurignacian across the whole of Europe from the Near East and Balkans to Iberia. Some Spanish archaeologists have even argued that the Aurignacian was a local development which then spread eastwards, but this is currently very much a minority view.

At the cutting edge: blade technology

The invention of blade technology is often cited as one of the principal defining features of the Upper Palaeolithic. Although this is not strictly true (blade-making is, for example, known in various Middle Palaeolithic industries), it is certainly the case that there was a sharp increase in the production of narrow, parallel-sided blades in this technology at the expense of flakes (see **13** and **75**).

One of the reasons for this shift in emphasis from flakes to blades seems to have been the increased reliance on hafted equipment. Just like the replaceable parts of a safety razor, standardized flint blades could easily be substituted in wooden and antler handles. Apart from labour saving (making the hafts was much more time-consuming than making new blades) this device also allowed a series of blades to be arranged in a row, thus considerably lengthening the available cutting edge. Recent discoveries of Middle Palaeolithic tools with hafting resins (glues) have shown that the use of handles was not a purely Upper Palaeolithic

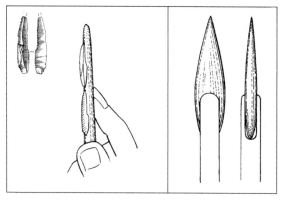

75 Upper Palaeolithic (Aurignacian) hafted equipment. Reconstruction of Dufour bladelets in a handle and a plain lozengic bone point in a shaft (not to scale).

99

phenomenon, but there can be little doubt that this became much more common in the Aurignacian with the introduction of smaller blade tools such as the Dufours and Font Yves bladelets (75).

In addition to the proliferation of small blade forms, there was also a noticeable increase in the overall range and variation of retouched stone tools. Much like the different components of a Swiss Army penknife each of the blades had a slightly different shape, linked to a specific function and together forming a multipurpose toolkit. Among the recognizable types were scrapers, borers, piercers and special chisel-ended implements known as burins (see 13). The existence of distinct sub-types in tools such as the burins indicates not only a diversity of specialist roles for this tool, but also implies well-practised skills in working ivory, antler and bone.

Abundant evidence linking blade tools, such as burins, with the carving of mammoth ivory, bone and deer antler can be found, for example, in the Aurignacian levels at the site of Geissenklosterle in south-western Germany. Typically high densities of bone and ivory debris show how these materials were cut, sawn, polished and ground into a remarkable diversity of forms. The distribution of manufacturing waste coincides with that of the flint burins, and microwear polishes on the edges of the tools confirm that they were extensively used for this purpose.

Coupled with the small blades, further indirect evidence for hafting comes from a variety of bone and ivory points with carefully modified bases (split, forked, bevelled). The points were characteristically made on long slender splinters removed from antler beams and/or mammoth tusks. The method required cutting deep parallel grooves with flint artefacts and prising out the splinter – giving rise to the term 'groove and splinter technique' (76). From the appearance of the points it is fairly clear that they were designed to fit onto the ends of wooden or antler shafts. The technology implies

they were used to tip composite throwing spears or short darts. To launch these weapons it is likely that spear-throwers or *atlatls* were employed (**colour plate 9**), although the earliest known evidence for these tools does not actually figure in the European record until about 18,000 years ago, in the Solutrean (77). Other contemporary throwing weapons may have included boomerangs. If the ivory tool from Oblazowa Cave (Poland) is correctly interpreted, it would suggest that returning weapons, accurate to within a distance of 200m (660ft), were already in use 20,000 years ago.

Improvements in hunting technology enabled weapons to be delivered with deadlier power and accuracy over greater distances, and this in turn allowed much more flexibility in hunting tactics. One of the advantages was that herd animals could be singled out and selectively culled, and groups of animals could be intercepted in larger numbers. Also connected with these changes was a shift towards the seasonal exploitation of game. This is borne out

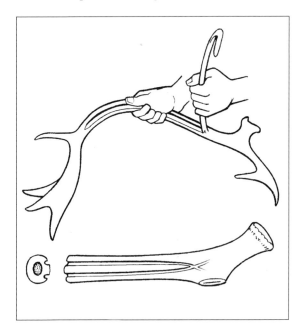

76 Groove-and-splinter technique on reindeer antler. Stone artefacts were used to gouge two parallel grooves before the central splinter was prised out by hand.

intensity occupation of short duration, again consistent with seasonal activities. As we have already seen in the Middle Palaeolithic, the hunting techniques of the Neanderthals were no less efficient but they were almost certainly not organized on a logistical basis. The introduction of new hunting strategies and an emphasis on seasonal patterns of exploitation were therefore among the key adaptive innovations of the Upper Palaeolithic.

Burial and personal ornaments

Human burial practices are well documented in the Early Upper Palaeolithic (Aurignacian and Gravettian), and reveal some significant differences with Neanderthal cultural traditions discussed in the previous chapter. For Cro-Magnons, the preferred custom of burial seems to have been inhumation but, unlike the Neanderthals, corpses were normally buried in a flat, extended position rather than lying crouched on one side.

Interesting differences also emerge in the arrangement of the corpses. Whereas Neanderthals buried their dead singly (there are one or two rare exceptions such as the double burial of two newborns at La Ferrassie, south-west France), modern humans were buried in single, double and multiple graves, and for the first time sometimes in pits out in the open as opposed to caves. The communal graves are particularly fascinating because they raise the issue of whether people had actually died at the same time or were incorporated separately, over time. In fact, it is clear that in certain cases, the dead were inserted together and this increases the likelihood of accidents or disease as explanatory causes. In two multiple graves from the Czech Republic studies of the skeletal material have revealed the close biological relationships between the dead. One of the burials, from Předmostí, is particularly intriguing because it contains the remains of twenty-nine individuals (thirteen adults, three sub-adults, and thirteen children). Only five individuals are represented by complete

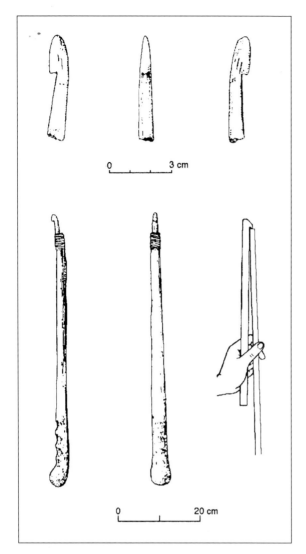

0 _____ 3 cm

0 _____ 20 cm

77 Upper Palaeolithic (Solutrean) spear-throwing hook of reindeer antler from Combe Saunière, south-west France. Below, an experimental reconstruction of a spear-thrower with its antler hook.

by faunal remains at French Upper Palaeolithic sites which reveal a preference for certain species, such as reindeer and horse, killed as they migrated *en masse* in the autumn and spring. Interestingly, a slightly different pattern of exploitation is demonstrated in south-western Germany where Aurignacian sites reveal a broader range of species, including mammoth, woolly rhino, horse, reindeer and ibex. But, as in the French sites, the evidence points to low skeletons (a figure not too dissimilar from other multiple burials of this period), the rest by small groups of bones or isolated body parts. The interpretation is complicated by the lack of detailed publication, but it seems that the bodies were piled up in the grave pit (4m by 2.5m/13ft by 8ft). However there are no signs of physical violence or post-mortem damage (except for one upper leg bone which seems to have defleshing marks) and so it has to be concluded that some natural catastrophe had overtaken them, assuming they all died within a short space of one another. An interesting angle is that Prédmostí and other large open-air sites like it

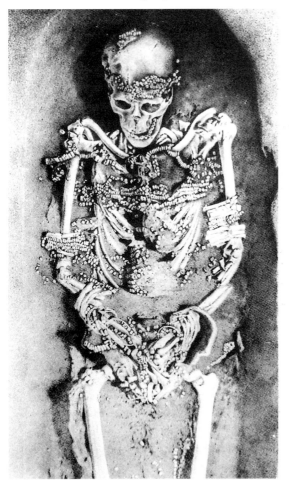

78 Upper Palaeolithic (Gravettian) burial dating to about 24,000 years ago from Sungir, Russia. An adult male was buried with ivory beads circling his head, wrists, elbows, knees and ankles.

are assumed to have been winter camps. It has been suggested by the archaeologist Alison Roberts that if people had perished over winter they may literally have been placed in cold storage (perhaps in snowdrifts) until the weather improved sufficiently to dig a proper grave. Alternatively, they may have been exhumed from graves dug over a longer time period. The cut-marked bone is a mysterious addition and may indicate that a cadaver was ritually skinned before it was buried.

A major distinction between modern human and Neanderthal burials is in the occurrence of grave goods. Although evidence from Prédmostí is peculiarly sparse (only a few pierced arctic fox teeth on a single skull), elsewhere in the Early Upper Palaeolithic burials are often accompanied by special grave goods. The contents of such graves may help give clues not only about rituals to the dead, but also about the day to day conditions of the living. For example, multiple and double burials in the Italian Riviera and on the Russian Steppes are wreathed in artefacts made of pierced animal teeth, ivory, marine shells, and fish vertebrae. From the position of these items, they were probably sewn onto clothing and head dresses and there is no reason to suppose that the wearing of tailored clothing was exclusively for the dead (78). Red ochre was often a common element. Sometimes the colorant covered the entire burial suggesting that it was sprinkled as powder over the corpse. Alternatively, it might have been used to dye garments in which the dead were wrapped. The rich symbolism of the blood-red colorant is self evident, but there may have been practical reasons for employing ochre as well, in controlling putrefaction of tissue and the smell of decay. This was probably not the reason for its use in the famous triple burial from Dolní Vestonice (Czech Republic), where ochre staining is localized on the skulls and in the pelvic region of the central skeleton (79).

For Clive Gamble, the ornaments worn by the dead were codified signs of status and gender of the individuals. But the objects are not

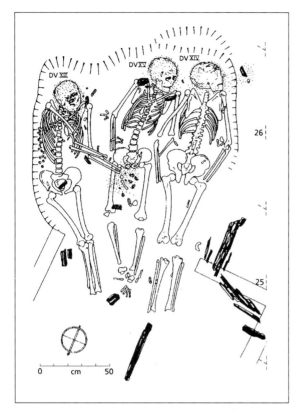

79 Upper Palaeolithic (Gravettian) triple burial from Dolní Vestonice, Moravia. The central individual (of uncertain sex) is flanked by two males both of whom had ivory pendants covering part of their skulls. Red ochre was scattered among the skulls and beneath the central individual's pelvis.

always employed in a consistent manner, which often makes them hard to decode. For example, items like flint knives (conventionally thought of as male objects) were found in the triple burial at Barme Grande (Italian Riviera) on the adult male and young female, but not on the young male in the same grave. Likewise 'female' objects such as jewellery and bracelets are not exclusively associated with female burials. The Palaeolithic specialist Paul Mellars has pointed out that the manufacture of ornaments in ivory and stone represents a considerable outlay of time and energy. This may imply the existence of craft specialization and could point to social differences between the wearers of these items. Similar ideas have been put forward by the American archaeologist Olga Soffer to explain stylistic differences in individual mammoth houses and pit contents of the Upper Palaeolithic hunters of Ukraine.

Art and decoration

The first appearance of complex representational art is one of the most dramatic signatures of the Early Upper Palaeolithic. European Palaeolithic art can be categorized according to whether it was portable (i.e. mobiliary) or appeared on rock walls (i.e. parietal). One of the finest examples of portable art is believed to be among the earliest, dating from bout 33,000–30,000 bp. It comes from Hohlenstein-Stadel in southern Germany and comprises an exquisite statuette of a male figure with a lion's head, carved out of mammoth ivory (80). Also from contemporary sites in southern Germany come highly ornate animal figures, carved in ivory and bone, and sometimes with incised markings on their bodies. Good examples of mammoth, bear and bison figures are known from the site of Geissenklosterle and reveal a breathtaking combination of technical expertise and powerful imagery. The famous female figurines (Venuses or Mother Goddesses) belong to the slightly later Gravettian phase of the Upper Palaeolithic from about 26,000 bp.

Any idea that the oldest wall art, as opposed to the first portable art, was extremely primitive has been completely dispelled by the recent discovery and dating of Chauvet Cave near Avignon, France. The cave art site discovered in 1994 reveals stylistically advanced wall paintings of animals that can be radiocarbon dated to about 31,000 bp. This not only places them firmly within the Aurignacian but makes them the oldest examples of representational wall art from anywhere in the world outside Australia. The sophistication of the techniques used at Chauvet implies a much longer tradition of experimentation and perfection, and it would be no surprise if even older examples were eventually to come to light in Europe.

80 Upper Palaeolithic (Aurignacian) ivory lion-headed statuette from Hohlenstein-Stadel, Germany. Height: 28.1cm (11in).

The interpretation of the art is a subject for a book in itself. Today, most archaeologists acknowledge that the visual symbols created on cave walls and portable objects encode complex cultural meanings and are not simply 'art for art's sake' or to do with 'hunting magic', as was believed in the past. While many of the messages behind the art lie beyond our present grasp, various intriguing and plausible suggestions can be offered by way of interpretation. One of the latest ideas to resurface is based on ethnographic evidence which suggests that the depiction of anthropomorphic figures (humans as animals), is linked with totemic religious beliefs and shamanism. Indeed David Lewis-Williams' study of the San of southern Africa has demonstrated conclusively a connection between hallucinatory images experienced during trancing and paintings made on rock walls. He draws parallels with Upper Palaeolithic art where so-called trance images (geometric and other abstract shapes known as 'entoptics') sometimes feature in the paintings. Occasionally, too, half animal/half human images, present in the southern African art, appear in European cave paintings (**81**). While this still does not explain all Upper Palaeolithic art (which is predominantly naturalistic with its portrayal of animals), the contribution of Lewis-Williams and others is extremely valuable because it highlights the multi-layered meanings behind ethnographic art and shows that Palaeolithic art can be understood at different levels simultaneously.

Expanded communication and exchange networks

The movement of objects over long distances is a distinctive feature of the Early Upper Palaeolithic and is probably indicative of advances in social organization and the development of greatly expanded communication networks. Among

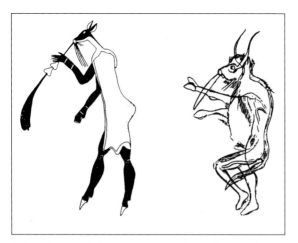

81 Half-animal, half-human figures (therianthropes) in South African rock art (left) and from Les Trois Frères, France (right). Both figures are apparently bleeding from the nose, which may occur during trance dancing.

transported items were tiny marine shells sometimes found hundreds of miles from their point of origin. Whether these objects were traded or exchanged or simply reflect the wide geographic range of early humans is not yet clear. Certainly evidence from Ukraine implies that such objects, as well as amber, were highly valued personal commodities often stored in large pits or found as grave goods adorning individual burials. Other far-travelled objects, such as fine-grained flints, were probably imported for their superior flaking properties over locally available materials. The long-distance movement of all these materials marks a complete break with the preceding Middle Palaeolithic traditions where such evidence is all but absent.

There are doubtless many reasons for the long distance transport of objects, but one plausible suggestion links it to the idea of group survival. According to this theory, Upper Palaeolithic human groups migrating into new regions would have been highly vulnerable, facing unknown and potentially hazardous conditions. In order to avoid the possibility of disaster – and even to allow an escape route if necessary – it was essential to maintain close

relations with even geographically distant neighbours. For Clive Gamble, the exchange of objects was a vital way of mediating social relationships over long distances. They provided the means of cementing and maintaining alliances with neighbouring groups. Or, to put it another way, such items symbolized an insurance policy: if food or other resources became scarce in one area, for example, the possession of common items of exchange and shared rituals, guaranteed access to other peoples' resources. A mutual support system of this kind was vital to the long-term survival of each colonizing group. While this explanation is reasonable enough, it makes it all the more extraordinary that earlier inhabitants of Europe, such as Neanderthals, coped so successfully for so long without the benefit of this strong cultural safety-net. It may, however, hint at one reason for their disappearance.

A superb example of the type of network envisaged is illustrated by the distribution of nearly identical ivory carvings of female figurines which were distributed on a pan-European scale between about 26,000 and 21,000 bp. According to Gamble, these figurines, often with exaggerated body proportions, may have been part of an unwritten code symbolizing common social ties and lines of exchange and communication. He believes it is no coincidence that figurines appeared at just the time when the climate began dipping into another intensely cold phase and food and other resources were becoming increasingly scarce.

Storage: insurance against food shortages

Another method of ensuring survival during leaner periods would have been to find an efficient means of storing food and other materials for future use. Evidence that some form of storage was employed by Cro-Magnons comes from two independent sources: cut-marked bones of meat animals and pits containing bones. Convincing examples of storage pits are admittedly hard to find in the archaeological record but some well-known instances have been recorded in the Ukraine. Here dwellings made of stacked mammoth bones are associated with pits, dug to the depth allowed by summer thawing of frozen ground. The pits are about 1.5–2m (5–6.5ft) in diameter, and up to 1m (3ft) deep, and the archaeologist Olga Soffer thinks that they were dug specifically with winter storage of meat in mind. From the distribution of finds within them, it appears that meaty segments were stored frozen on the bone, packed between layers of silty clay. Other pits, with a more chaotic arrangement of bones, have been interpreted as rubbish pits, backfilled with food remains.

Bones at many Upper Palaeolithic sites reveal butchery traces. The cut-marks are consistent with filleting of meat and its removal off the bone. This has led to speculation that the thin strips of meat were then smoked or dried for storage purposes, although by definition this activity is virtually invisible from an archaeological point of view. Based on observations of ethnographic hunter-gatherers it seems that apart from the processing time, which is lengthy, curing provides a relatively efficient, low bulk method of meat storage. For mobile Upper Palaeolithic hunters, it would have had the added benefit of conserving meat in a highly portable form, ideal for transportation purposes.

Hearths

Well-built fireplaces are a standard component of Upper Palaeolithic sites. Rather than simple ash spreads or shallow charcoal-filled depressions, hearths became structurally more complex, often incorporating stone borders and sometimes even stone-linings. Such features undoubtedly made them much more efficient both in terms of conducting and conserving heat. These improvements may have been linked to specific uses. Certainly, much later in the Upper Palaeolithic (about 13,000 bp) there is good evidence of large stone cooking slabs associated with fireplaces. Despite changes in hearth structure, it should be emphasized that flat or scooped campfires (identical to Neanderthal examples) are known to have continued in existence, side by side with stone built constructions, throughout the Upper Palaeolithic.

The appearance of more sophisticated hearth construction is mirrored by the greater attention apparently given to the location and spacing of hearths in given situations. For example, at the Abri Pataud (south-western France), in the Aurignacian level dating to 32,000 years ago, the hearths appear to have been deliberately arranged in a neat row near the back wall of the shelter. This pattern is interpreted by Lewis Binford as marking the positions of individual sleeping spaces, each person nestling snugly between two hearths. While it is hard not to read too much into this kind of evidence, there are increasing signs in the Upper Palaeolithic of social activities focusing on the fireplace. Drawing upon concentric distribution patterns of artefacts and other materials scattered around hearths Clive Gamble is convinced that modern humans, unlike Neanderthals, were spending much more of their time socializing at the fireside: chatting and exchanging vital information or simply engaging in story-telling. But hearths also fulfilled a range of practical functions, less common in earlier periods, as for example in preparing mastic and resins for gluing flint and organic tools into projectile shafts. Small oven-like hearths were employed at Dolní Vestonice for baking clay figurines.

Language and the modern mind

The explosion of artistic creativity in the Upper Palaeolithic has been likened to the 'big bang' of human culture. For archaeologist Steven Mithen these new developments were a direct consequence of intellectual advances which were themselves made possible by changes to the inner workings of the mind. Whereas in earlier hominids the mind consisted of a number of separate specialized intelligences working in isolation, the modern brain brought much greater fluidity between each of these domains (see **62**). This literally transformed the human mind, enabling knowledge from the different cognitive spheres (social, technical and natural history intelligence) to be shared and become fully interactive. In short, it was this merging of the mind which created the enormous stimulus for creative change.

Explaining the actual process of change is rather more complicated, but Mithen has come up with the proposition that, around 500,000 years ago, increased brain size provided the initial starting point. Related to brain enlargement was the development of what he calls 'social language', which gradually switched to a more 'general purpose language' capable of transmitting all sorts of non-social information, and allowing individuals to acquire much greater flexibility, sensitivity and creativity in their conscious minds. The context for these latest changes appears to have been an increase in the time between birth and maturity. This extended period of infancy and childhood is a characteristic which distinguishes ourselves from archaic humans, such as the Neanderthals. A more gradual period of brain growth and development in Cro-Magnon children would have given more time for their intellectual abilities to emerge.

A key issue in the emergence of modern behaviour is the question of language development and its origins. As we have discussed in previous chapters, it is likely that archaic humans, including the Boxgrove people, had some capacity for language even if it was of a very rudimentary nature. The argument for Neanderthals possessing linguistic skills is much stronger, but here again the evidence points to more limited abilities compared with modern people, both in the sense of producing speech sounds and in thinking capacity. Thus, the decisive transition to complex syntactic language is invariably focused on modern humans, but did this happen immediately or only after anatomically modern humans had colonized Europe and other parts of the Old World?

From an archaeological perspective, the first anatomically modern people do not seem very advanced culturally. In fact the burials of moderns at Qafzeh (Israel) dating to 90,000 years ago, are remarkably similar to Neanderthal burials of the same age, with few if any grave goods. During this period there are no discernible changes in technology; tools recognizable as Mousterian occur both with early moderns at Skhūl (Israel) and their Neanderthal contemporaries at Tabun (Israel). And although moderns may have had the upper hand in predicting the seasonal movements of gazelle, they continued to use the same hunting equipment as Neanderthals. For many archaeologists therefore, the crucial turning point came thousands of years after the first appearance of anatomically modern humans. As we have seen, the transition can be dated to around 40,000–30,000 bp in western Europe with the explosion in creative expression and complex symbolic behaviour (e.g. art and decorated burial), but it probably happened earlier elsewhere. Whatever it was that shaped human behaviour in this way, it seems inconceivable that the ability to symbolize thoughts and to think abstractly could have happened without complex language. The inescapable conclusion is that language had a pivotal role in the Upper Palaeolithic revolution.

The last surviving Neanderthals and their industries

The apparent suddenness with which modern humans burst on to the European scene cannot properly be assessed without reference to the fate of the Neanderthals. As mentioned earlier, there seems little doubt that modern human populations moved into western Europe about 40,000 years ago and replaced the Neanderthals. But it is also important to realize that the Neanderthals, for their part, did not simply disappear overnight. In fact there is good evidence that they survived, albeit in isolated pockets in southern Spain, until about 30,000 years ago. Such a situation might have allowed

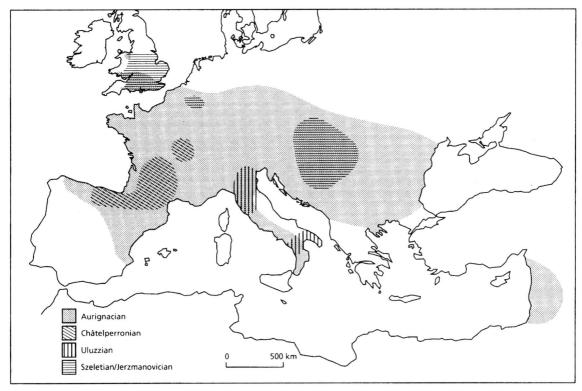

82 Geographical distribution of Early Upper Palaeolithic industries in Europe (including the Near East).

considerable interaction between the two human populations but there is surprisingly little evidence in support of this. Instead, current thinking favours the view that the archaic people were outcompeted by the moderns and were gradually forced into living in marginal environments. This does not mean the Neanderthals were hunted to extinction, rather that they were simply sidelined by their more advanced neighbours. In their book *African Exodus* Stringer and McKie present a bleak picture of the last surviving Neanderthals: 'Their access to good foraging and hunting ranges was reduced, their interchange of mates disrupted, and their ability to maintain population numbers seriously curtailed.' In their view extinction was a long, slow inexorable process which took over 10,000 years.

But what actually happened during this 10,000-year period of overlap? What cultural evidence would we expect to find of the last

surviving Neanderthals and how is it relevant to the British archaeological record?

There is little disagreement that the Early Upper Palaeolithic Aurignacian marks a distinct break with the Mousterian. The uniformity of appearance and widespread distribution of the Aurignacian also conforms with the idea of new ideas being transmitted by incoming populations (**82**). Here, however, the consensus largely ends. The picture is also complicated by the existence of distinctive industries in this 10,000-year period that do not fit comfortably into either the Aurignacian or the Mousterian.

One of the industries concerned – the Châtelperronian – has little or no relevance to the British record and will be mentioned only in passing. It has been found in direct association with Neanderthal fossils at St Césaire, south-western France (dating to 36,000 bp), at Arcy-sur-Cure (dating to 34,000 bp) and at a number of other locations in northern Spain. For many French archaeologists the Châtelperronian (or Lower Perigordian) is an interesting hybrid because it combines Middle Palaeolithic tools with Upper Palaeolithic traditions of blade-making and a developed bone industry. Previously, the most favoured explanation was one of acculturation. It was believed that Neanderthals had come into contact with moderns and had literally copied the Aurignacian technology during the period of coexistence. Archaeologists Lawrence Straus and Paul Pettitt, however, are more sceptical. They have noted, independently, major differences in raw material use between the Aurignacian and Mousterian and this has led Pettitt to suggest that the French Châtelperronian assemblages are simply mixtures of the two technologies, creating an artificial hybrid.

Another industry which may have emerged from the local Mousterian is the Szeletian/Jerzmanovician of central and eastern Europe (82). This tradition, which incorporates the so-called 'leaf point' industries, is of interest because it extends as far west as the British Isles. The geographic distribution of the leaf point tradition is more restricted than the Aurignacian but they seem to have overlapped in time. However, since no human fossils have yet been found in association with leaf points, any link with the last Neanderthals is still highly conjectural.

Early Upper Palaeolithic in Britain

At least three different sub-divisions of the Early Upper Palaeolithic can be recognized in Britain on the basis of artefact typology. According to Roger Jacobi, two of them have recognizable equivalents in the classic French sequence but the third, and earliest, seems to be more closely related to the eastern European leaf point traditions. Detailed information on the dating and sequence of the British industries is extremely scanty and there is an undoubted need for further scientific enquiry.

Phase 1: Beedings and Jerzmanovice leaf points

The first of these technologies is characterized by bifacial and unifacial leaf points, which may themselves belong to independent traditions.

The latter (**colour plate 10**) are similar to examples found at the Polish cave of Nietoperzowa near the town of Jerzmanovice. These are made on blades with a triangular cross-section and pointed at one end. The blade-points are unifacially retouched with the chipping on the ventral surface and frequently limited to the extremities. There can be little doubt that the points were intended for hafting because the secondary retouch serves to straighten the natural curvature of the blades and to thin them. Although probably too large (and too early in time) for arrowheads, the points would have made excellent spear tips, an observation further emphasized by the fact that several examples found at British sites carry impact fractures on their tips.

Currently, about twenty-two findspots with Jerzmanovice points are known in Britain (83). All but one of them (Ffynnon Beuno, north

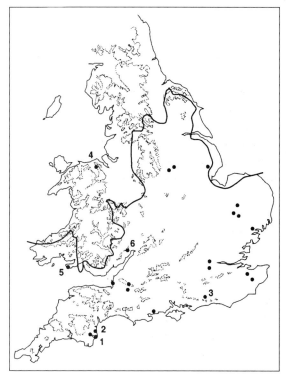

83 Distribution of Jerzmanovice leaf blade-points. Site names: 1 Bench Tunnel Cavern, 2 Kent's Cavern, 3 Pulborough (Beedings), 4 Ffynnon Beuno Cave, 5 Paviland Cave, 6 King Arthur's Cave.

Wales) is south of the limit of maximum ice advance in the last glaciation which implies that further sites in the north might have been lost due to the destructive effects of ice movements. Leaf points have been found both in caves and open-air sites.

The dating of Jerzmanovice assemblages is still very unclear. A date of 38,560 ± 1,250 bp has been obtained from the lowest level with leaf points at the type site of Nietoperzowa cave. In Britain at Bench Tunnel Cavern (Brixham, Devon), a Jerzmanovice point was found beneath a hyena mandible dating to 34,500 ± 1,400 bp. Although not dating the point itself, it provides a minimum age for the artefact, which broadly falls within the earliest part of the age range for such points at other sites in the east and on the Russian Plain e.g. Kostienki-Streletskaya. These dates of course overlap with both the Aurignacian and various industries attributed to the last Neanderthals.

By far the largest collection of finds from this period in Britain comes from a site at Beedings (83), near Pulborough (Sussex), which has produced thirty-three flint leaf points. The flints, recovered in 1900, were recorded as coming from sand pockets (fissures or gulls) in the Lower Greensand bedrock, presumably having been washed in from an ancient landsurface. The surviving assemblage consisted mainly of broken leaf points and retouched tools made on the ends of leaf points.

Recent re-analysis of these finds has led Roger Jacobi to some interesting conclusions about the artefacts. First, the leaf points are not on locally-occurring flint, which means they were probably not made at the site. From the profiles of the tools it is clear they had been made on blades deliberately straightened and pointed by partial surface chipping, which also served to 'thin' them down. The reasons are quite clear according to Jacobi: they were spear tips brought to the site in wooden spearshafts. Since some of the points had 'impact fractures' at the tips he concludes that Beedings was a temporary hunting fieldstation where broken

projectile equipment was dismantled and repaired. In the absence of suitable local raw materials, the smashed points were not simply thrown away but were recycled into other tools such as end-scrapers and burins (84).

Phase 2: Aurignacian II, Kent's Cavern and the Paviland Cave burial

Following the early appearance of modern humans in southern Europe there may have been a considerable time lag, of several thousand years, before any populations were established in north-western Europe, including Britain. The colonization of this region seems to have been delayed until about 33,000–30,000 bp, and paradoxically, one of the most securely dated human fossils of this period comes from Britain, on the extreme periphery of this region. The partial upper jaw (see 74) from Kent's Cavern, Devon, was found during excavations of the Vestibule inside the cave in the 1920s. AMS radiocarbon dating on the specimen has provided an age of 30,900 ± 900 bp.

According to Jacobi, the Kent's Cavern human jaw was reported as coming from beneath a 'stalagmite floor' or similar natural pavement. Unfortunately there were no diagnostic tools in this level so the cultural associations of the jaw are uncertain. Of the two likeliest affiliations both Jerzmanovice leaf points and tools of Aurignacian II type (the second earliest Aurignacian sub-phase) occurred in the cave, but according to Dorothy Garrod, the leading Upper Palaeolithic expert of the day, leaf points were absent in the Vestibule itself. It is therefore possible that the human remains were linked with the Aurignacian II industry, though, since the Aurignacian artefacts were recorded above the stalagmite floor, the association cannot be proven.

Another important early modern human fossil comes from Paviland Cave (formerly Goats Hole), on the Gower Peninsula in South Wales (85). The find was that of a spectacular burial of an adult male covered in red ochre and accompanied by numerous grave goods. It was

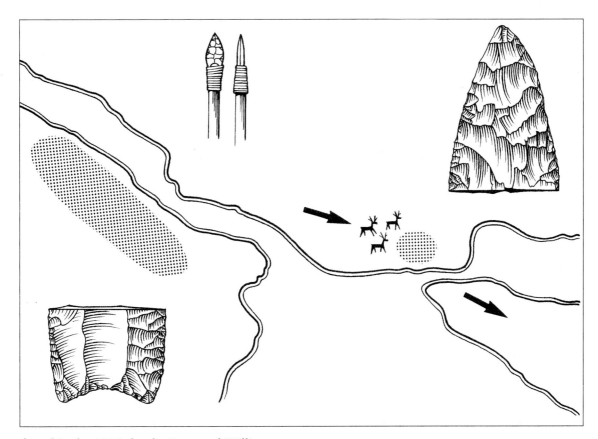

found in the 1820s by the Reverend William Buckland, a great eccentric and the first professor of mineralogy and geology at Oxford University. Published details of the discovery make it clear that the skeleton lay in a shallow grave (86), in an extended position not far from the cave entrance. The burial had been partly damaged by erosion and the skull and most of the right side of the body were missing. Nevertheless, enough of the original grave was preserved to show extensive red ochre staining on the bones and surrounding sediment. The prolific use of ochre was noted by the excavator who remarked that it extended 'about half an inch around the surface of the bones'. Accompanying the burial were the fragments of slender mammoth ivory bracelets and rods lying in contact with the body's ribs and 'two handsfull' of small perforated Periwinkle sea shells heaped neatly in a pile on the thigh. The objects were stained the same bright red colour as the bones.

84 Vail, Maine (USA), a parallel for Beedings (Sussex)? Palaeoindians used stone fluted spear points to hunt caribou (reindeer). Reconstruction of the Vail site shows that the animals were ambushed and killed as they crossed the river. Evidence comes from fluted spear tips with 'impact fractures'. Some of the broken tips can be refitted to the basal fragments found at another location about 225m (250 yards) away. Interpretation suggests that because suitable rock-types were scarce locally, the broken stubs were carried back to the site for recycling into other tools. A similar situation exists at Beedings where new tools have been refashioned out of broken points. Unlike Vail, however, the kill site has not been located.

In the original report the skeleton was mistakenly described as female and ceremoniously dubbed the 'Red Lady' of Paviland. Much later, it was established that the burial was of a young male adult about twenty-five years old and 1.7m (5ft 7in) tall – but by then it was too late, the name had become

85 The 1912 Sollas excavations in progress at Paviland Cave, Gower.

firmly embedded in the literature. Moreover, since nineteenth-century religious views did not accept the coexistence of humans and extinct animals, like mammoth, no one at the time suspected the true antiquity of the find. Indeed, Buckland resolutely believed that the burial was of Roman age, and whether or not an elaborate pun was intended (Buckland was a notorious prankster), the skeleton was regarded, quite literally, as that of a 'scarlet woman' (prostitute) attached to a nearby Roman soldiers' camp!

Despite general acceptance that the burial was Upper Palaeolithic, controversy has continued to surround the dating of the skeleton. Radiocarbon tests carried out by Kenneth Oakley in 1968 revealed that it was

just over 18,000 years old, within the Last Glacial Maximum (LGM), when much of northern Europe was covered with ice. More recently, bone powder taken from the tibia has been redated to 26,350 ± 550 bp and, under the circumstances, seems a more realistic estimate. However, the new date still does not resolve matters entirely, as we shall see below.

A further source of uncertainty concerns whether or not the cave served as a place of both the living and the dead. Logic would imply that the great majority of non-flint artefacts belonged to a highly elaborate burial since similar ornaments are known from other Upper Palaeolithic inhumations. Among the items recovered were over forty fragments of ivory rods and parts of two ivory bracelets (**86**), all ochre-stained and apparently found with the skeleton. The cylindrical ivory rods were either parts of ceremonial wands or blanks for beads that were never completed. One piece of ivory was decorated with engraved lines. An interesting feature of the sea shells are the perforations which imply they were sewn onto clothing or were suspended from necklaces or bracelets. In contrast to these ornaments, Buckland also recovered plenty of evidence to suggest that manufacturing activities took place inside the cave. These included broken or unfinished ivory tools, as well as the skull and tusk fragment of a mammoth. Corroborating these observations were the findings of W. J. Sollas who conducted further investigations of the cave in 1912. He found a pierced egg-shaped ivory pendant (**colour plate 11**) made on a growth caused by a wound which matched a depression in the tusk found by Buckland. Of less certain association were several large slabs of limestone reported by Sollas and believed by him to have been placed at the head and feet of the corpse at the time of burial.

Ultimately, these two apparently conflicting interpretations of burial vs. ivory workshop need not prove contradictory. For example, what if the cave had been the destination of an ivory-hunting expedition that had gone

86 Reconstruction of the 'Red Lady' burial at Paviland Cave.

disastrously wrong? Imagine a situation in which one member of the team died unexpectedly, a long way from home, or had been mortally injured in a hunting accident (though there were no signs of violence on any part of the skeleton). In these circumstances, it would not be surprising to find signs of occupation debris mixed in with evidence of burial activity. There also seems little doubt that the manufacture of ivory objects far exceeded the number of grave goods recovered. From the size of the tusk found it is clear that many items must have been removed when the expedition finally left the cave. If this is the case then it seems hardly likely that all the activities were linked to the burial.

New work at the site in 1997, by archaeologist Stephen Aldhouse-Green, will hopefully clarify the cultural associations of the burial. Until now this has been difficult to ascertain because of the wide range of typological evidence found in the cave. The bulk of the retouched stone tools are identifiable as Aurignacian II (**87**). They include characteristic nosed-scrapers, straight scrapers and busked (notched-stopped) burins. Identical artefacts are also known from Kent's Cavern (Devon), and a small number of other locations in Britain (**88**). No secure dates are yet available for this industry, though on the basis of continental parallels an age in the range of 32,000–30,000 bp would be expected. This means, of course, that the burial is probably of younger age.

Perhaps as Roger Jacobi has perceptively remarked: 'a cave for the dead may not be a

87 Early Upper Palaeolithic artefacts from Paviland. Left to right: Leaf blade-point, busked burin, two scrapers and the tang of a Font Robert point.

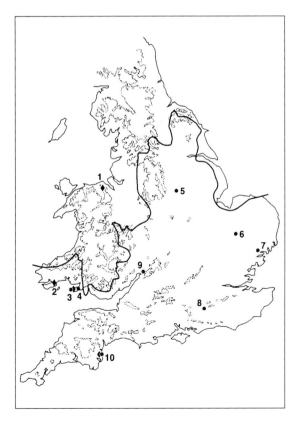

base for the living'. Paviland certainly had multiple phases of occupation and these probably indicate human uses of varying length and intensity over an extremely long timespan. According to this view the cave could have been used on many separate occasions either for burial or temporary accommodation, but never during the same period.

Phase 3: Font Robert points and the Gravettian

Evidence of another typologically distinct Early Upper Palaeolithic industry also occurs at Paviland. It includes artefacts of Gravettian (or Upper Perigordian) type. Typical of this phase are large tanged points with surface dorsal retouch (87). Analogous examples have been found at several other British sites (88). Based on the European sequence, parallels for these tools appear in assemblages from about 28,000

88 Distribution of findspots of Aurignacian II (diamond symbols) and Gravettian Font Robert points (dot symbols). 1 Ffynnon Beuno Cave, 2 Hoyle's Mouth Cave, 3 Paviland Cave, 4 Cat Hole Cave, 5 Pin Hole Cave, 6 Mildenhall, 7 Ipswich (Bramford Road), 8 Godalming (Peper Harow Park), 9 Barnwood (Forty Acre Field Pit), 10 Kent's Cavern.

to 22,000 bp and therefore offer better agreement with the age of the Paviland burial.

Despite current uncertainty over the cultural affinities of the Paviland adult, it seems clear that his group was operating on the extreme edge of the geographic range exploited by European Early Upper Palaeolithic hunter-gatherers. The period between 30,000 and 25,000 bp was one of rapid climatic oscillation (see Chapter 2). It is quite likely therefore that each of the milder episodes indicated in the ice core record saw temporary incursions of human groups onto the British peninsula.

In the above paragraphs some of the current ideas on the Early Upper Palaeolithic have been reviewed and its cultural characteristics considered in relation to the Middle Palaeolithic. The main thrust of the argument has been that modern human populations were responsible for introducing a new type of material culture into Europe between 40,000 and 30,000 bp. The nature of the transition was also briefly considered. This is a subject where fresh breakthroughs are now urgently required. The British sequence illustrates some of the problems in weighing up the key thresholds in human evolution (the replacement of Neanderthals by modern humans) and relating them to cultural changes in the archaeological record.

8

Britain at the end of the last Ice Age

A gap in human settlement

During the coldest part of the last cold stage, around 18,000 years ago, much of northern Europe, including Britain, seems to have been deserted by people. The period, known as the Last Glacial Maximum (LGM), is marked by renewed expansion of regional ice sheets which reached several kilometres thick in Scotland (**89**) and allowed lobes of ice to penetrate as far south as Glamorgan and Norfolk. During this time Britain was turned into a polar landscape devoid of animals and plants except the hardiest tundra species which were largely restricted to the south of the country. Fossil beetle evidence indicates that mean annual temperatures dropped to a minimum of –6° to –7°C, colder even than some parts of Siberia today. A further indication of the freezing conditions comes from marine micro-organisms which show surface sea temperatures cold enough for pack ice to develop off the north coast of Spain.

Even though no evidence for settlement in Britain exists, it is clear that Europe was not abandoned altogether. Archaeological data from this period reveal several major clusters of sites south of the River Loire in France and Spain and further east along the rivers of Ukraine. These locations seem to have acted as human refuges through the coldest phases of the last glaciation. There are no detailed population statistics but some estimates (based on site density and distribution) suggest relatively high levels of occupation – between 2,000 and 3,000

people living in southern France and Spain (roughly one person per 20km²/8 square miles). In the tundra zones to the north very much lower figures might be anticipated (perhaps only one person per 200km²/77 square miles) but in any case there is very little proof that these environments were ever inhabited except on a sporadic basis.

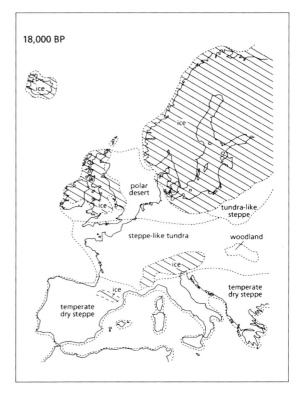

89 Reconstructed vegetational patterns for the Last Glacial Maximum (LGM), around 18,000 bp.

Table 7 *British and European subdivisions of the Lateglacial, 13,000–10,000 years ago.*

C years BP	Pollen zones	NW European chronozones	NW European climatostratigraphic units	British Stages
	IV	PREBOREAL	FLANDRIAN	FLANDRIAN
10,000				
	III	YOUNGER DRYAS	Transition	LOCH LOMOND STADIAL
			YOUNGER DRYAS STADIAL	
11,000				
	II	ALLERØD	Transition	
11,800				
	Ic	OLDER DRYAS		
12,000				WINDERMERE INTERSTADIAL
	Ib			
		BØLLING	LATEGLACIAL INTERSTADIAL	
13,000				
		MIDDLE WEICHSELIAN	Transition	DIMLINGTON STADIAL

Recolonization of Britain after the LGM

Exactly when and how Britain and the rest of northern Europe were resettled after the LGM is currently a subject of much speculation. Once the climate had improved sufficiently (see below) there were no obvious impediments to recolonization, and yet there seems to have been a considerable time lag before signs of sustained human activity can be recognized in our own archaeological record.

According to one model proposed by archaeologists Rupert Housley, Martin Street and Clive Gamble, human groups would have spread northwards into unoccupied areas of Europe by a series of leapfrogging migrations. Theoretically, in each case, it began with an early 'pioneer' phase in which small numbers of individuals initially migrated into empty areas; this was then followed by a more prolonged 'residential' phase marked by the areas becoming increasingly populated. The model is at present only based on a thin scatter of radiocarbon dates but it suggests that a founding wave of colonizers arrived in Britain around 12,600 bp, some 500 years later than the adjacent Continent and, perhaps, fully 1,000 radiocarbon years after eastern and south-

western Germany. However, some people suspect these data have been 'overinterpreted', and, for my own part, I see no definite evidence yet in Britain of distinct pioneer and residential phases of colonization. Indeed, using the same data one could reasonably argue that much of northern Europe was resettled simultaneously, leaving only the peripheral zones (like Britain) to be populated at a later time. Moreover, based on long distance mobility patterns it is conceivable that human groups moved in and out of Britain on a seasonal basis, rather than following the suggested pattern of successive phases.

Lateglacial environments

The end of the last cold stage is marked by a series of climatic oscillations referred to as the Lateglacial (Windermere) Interstadial and (Loch Lomond) Stadial (see **Table 7**). The first of these oscillations resulted in a dramatic climb in temperatures, which reached their peak around 13,000 years ago when the climate became as warm, if not warmer, than it is today. Following this climatic optimum, temperatures steadily declined until the interstadial ended about 11,000 years ago. During the ensuing stadial renewed glacier expansion took place in the Scottish Highlands but terminated around 10,000 years ago, marking the start of the present interglacial.

The currently accepted view is that Britain was re-occupied from Europe during the Windermere Interstadial but was abandoned again in the following Loch Lomond Stadial. Recent reviews of the evidence suggest that initial recolonization of Britain took place around 12,600 bp after the warm optimum, when the climate was already on the downturn. This has been explained in terms of a human time-lag in reaching Britain from the adjacent Continent, but dating evidence from France and Belgium, of about 13,000 bp, suggests that the picture might be more complicated. The phase of temperature decline in Britain is marked by a gradual change from open vegetation (grassland with sedges and willows) to more closed habitats (juniper and dwarf birch, followed by developed birch woodland after 12,000 bp) (**90**). The end of the Windermere Interstadial is

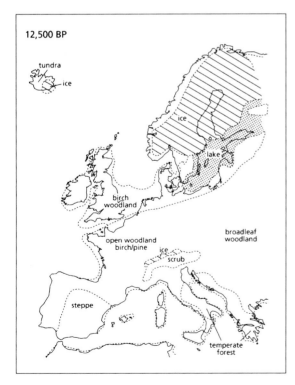

90 Reconstructed vegetational patterns for the Lateglacial interstadial, around 12,500 bp.

signalled by a rapid fall in average annual temperatures and the re-appearance of typical open tundra plant species, after about 11,000 years ago. According to the ice core data (**91**) the return to a more glacial climate seems to have occurred remarkably quickly, perhaps within as little as a single human generation.

Despite the fluctuating climate and vegetational changes, the native animal species remained remarkably stable throughout the interstadial. Among the dominant large vertebrates were horse and red deer, while other species included mammoth, wild cattle, elk, wolf, red fox, arctic fox and brown bear (**92**). The presence of Siberian animals like saiga antelope in the earlier half of the Windermere may suggest that conditions were at times more continental than today, while the extinction of mammoth in Britain seems to coincide with disappearance of more open habitats in the second half of the interstadial (after 12,000 bp). One surprising absentee in the contemporary British faunas is reindeer which was one of the dominant animals in the European Lateglacial record. Its absence in Britain may have been for climatic reasons, a view strengthened by its dramatic reappearance after 11,000 bp, following the return of much drier and colder stadial conditions. Other signs of climatic deterioration in the Loch Lomond Stadial may be found in the presence of cold climatic indicators among small mammal faunas. A good example is provided by the well-dated sequence at King Arthur's Cave (Herefordshire) which contains evidence of reindeer, as well as collared and Norway lemming, and narrow-skulled vole (**colour plates 12**, **13** and **14**, and **93**). The nearest equivalent habitats of these species today are in Scandinavia.

People and burials

Direct evidence of Lateglacial humans comes from their burials. In Britain the most famous example is from Gough's Cave, in the Cheddar Gorge, Somerset. Here, excavations in the 1890s and more recently in 1986–7 (**94**), uncovered

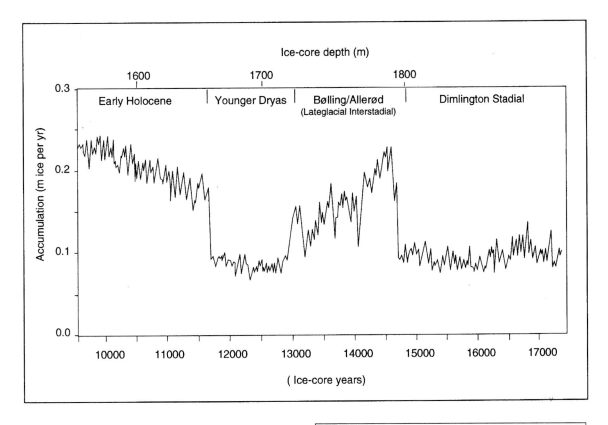

Ice-core depth (m)

91 Temperature curve derived from the Greenland Ice Core with the equivalent stages of the land-based pollen record. The gradual cooling trend and various small-scale oscillations at the end of the interstadial are all plainly visible in the Greenland Ice Core data.

92 Lateglacial interstadial fauna. Top left, clockwise: wolf, arctic fox, wild horse, aurochs, saiga antelope, red deer, mammoth, brown bear, arctic hare (not to scale).

the remains of at least three adults and two children, the latter aged between about 11–13 years and 3–5 years respectively. The skeletal evidence is well preserved, and this has allowed a range of scientific tests to be carried out on the bones and teeth including radiocarbon dating and, latterly, some exciting new work on ancient DNA analysis. The remarkable completeness of the bones has also enabled a detailed study to be made of the how the bodies were prepared for disposal. This has provided some unexpected surprises for archaeologists as we shall see below.

Analysis of the Gough's Cave bones has confirmed that the people were physically modern-looking and belonged to our own species of *Homo sapiens sapiens*. Direct AMS dates on the bones show roughly when the people died but because they cover a relatively wide radiocarbon timespan (11,800–12,400 bp) it is not clear whether this is due to standard measurement error or the fact that the deaths were widely spaced in time. Although detailed evidence is lacking on the original finds, information from the recently excavated human material suggests it was possibly a midden deposit rather than a formal grave. This is because it was found mixed up with other debris of domestic activity including animal bones and flint artefacts, as well as antler and ivory tools (95).

93 Vertical section through the Lateglacial sequence of deposits outside King Arthur's Cave (Herefordshire). Cold deposits (angular limestone) containing lemmings and reindeer overlie warm interstadial deposits (darker limestone sediments above scale bars) with red deer and Final Upper Palaeolithic artefacts.

94 Interior of Gough's Cave (Somerset) near the entrance showing the 1986–7 excavation area.

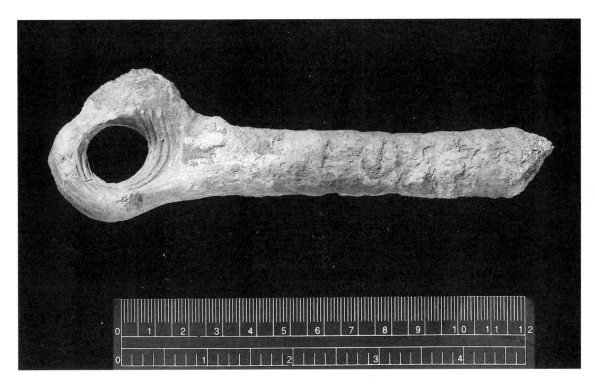

95 One of three reindeer antler bâtons from Gough's Cave.

An interesting new approach to studying skeletons of this age has come from the work of Brian Sykes, Martin Richards and their colleagues at Oxford University. It concerns the extraction of ancient genetic material from specimens of bone collagen and tooth dentine. The principle is well known. It relies on the idea that one type of DNA (mtDNA) is inherited exclusively through the maternal line and the rate of natural mutation and divergence from the parent mtDNA occurs at a predictable rate over time. Using small quantities of tooth dentine from the individuals at Gough's Cave, the Oxford group have been attempting to build a genetic profile of Britain's Lateglacial inhabitants. By estimating the number of mutations that have accumulated in mtDNA through time, and comparing individual genetic sequences, they may one day be able to infer a direct link between present-day Europeans and people who lived in the Cheddar Gorge 12,000 years ago. So far their results have been inconclusive but the signs are optimistic and this is an area in which major advances are eagerly anticipated.

A further insight into the human occupants of Gough's Cave comes from a more conventional study of the bones. Here, work carried out by archaeologist Jill Cook has revealed an astonishing collection of cut-marks on various skeletal elements of the body (**96**). Microscopic analysis of the cuts and scrapes reveal that they were made with flint knives, after the individuals had died. The position of the marks shows that the cadavers had been expertly skinned and the joints dismembered probably soon after death. Incisions on the inside of one of the jaws even revealed how the tongue had been carefully detached from the mouth.

Such activities today may strike us as macabre in the extreme but they are by no means unique in the archaeological or ethnohistoric records. In the ethnographic literature there are examples of two-stage burials: bodies were first placed on exposure platforms for defleshing and then collected for interment elsewhere. Sometimes, as in the case of some New Guinea groups, tradition

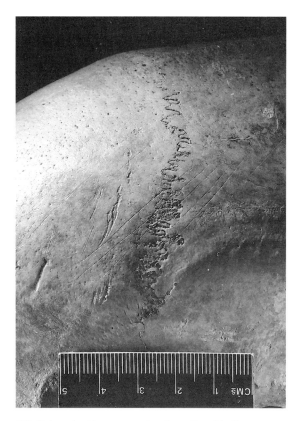

96 Cut-marked human cranium from Gough's Cave.

demanded that the soft tissues of the brain were ritually consumed before burial. Although we may never know the exact circumstances surrounding the burials at Gough's Cave it is likely that a two-stage process was involved: a first stage in which the corpse was dismembered followed either by the scattering of bones or collecting them in hide sacks and neatly arranging them against the walls of the cave. There is no convincing evidence for the consumption of human flesh, either ritually or as a substitute for other food. Indeed, judging from the large quantities of smashed and burnt animal bone found in the cave, it is likely that any feasting that did take place, was on haunches of venison rather than human flesh.

Late Upper Palaeolithic and Final Palaeolithic material culture

The tools and artefacts of this period are classified as Late Upper Palaeolithic and Final Upper Palaeolithic, as distinct from cultural finds from the period before the LGM (as discussed in the preceding chapter). One major industrial tradition is recognizable within the British Late Upper Palaeolithic, the Creswellian, named after the Creswell Crags, on the Derbyshire–Nottinghamshire border. The Final Upper Palaeolithic is less easy to define because of its overall diversity but includes a 'penknife-point' phase and a 'long blade' phase.

The Creswellian industry appears to be a late regional variant of the Magdalenian, a very widespread cultural tradition found over large parts of Lateglacial Europe. The British industry differs slightly on the grounds of tool typology. Whereas the French and Belgian Late Magdalenian contains straight-backed blades and bladelets, the characteristic backed tool of the Creswellian is the Cheddar point (**colour plate 15** and **97**). Damage found along the margins of these trapezoidal blades suggests they were used as knives rather than points, so the term 'point' has little functional relevance.

Despite these differences, the Creswellian shares many characteristics with its European counterparts. For instance, flint scrapers and burins are made on the ends of long blades, and the blade manufacturing technique is identical to that of the French Late Magdalenian. Moreover, close parallels can also be found among the non-lithic artefacts, including some made on mammoth ivory, such as the double-bevelled rods from Gough's Cave (Somerset) and Kent's Cavern (Devon). Reindeer antler was used to make bâtons at Gough's Cave (see **95**), and scooped-end rods at Fox Hole (Derbyshire) and Church Hole (Creswell Crags, Nottinghamshire). Products of antler also include three barbed harpoons from Kent's Cavern (**98**), while leg bones of arctic hare modified for use as pointed awls have been recovered at Gough's Cave and Robin Hood Cave (Creswell Crags, Derbyshire). Other organic items include bone needles at Gough's Cave, Church Hole and Kent's Cavern, plus an awl – though not of hare bone – from the latter

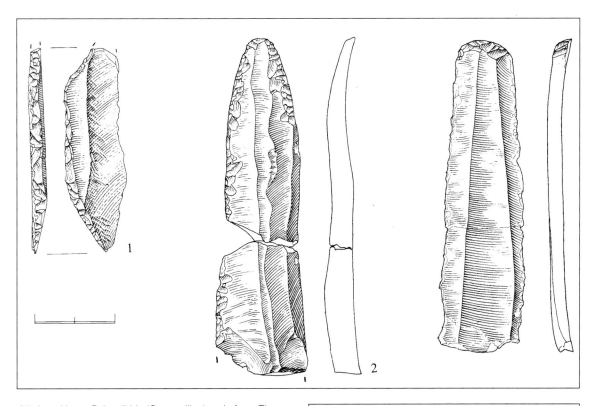

97 Late Upper Palaeolithic (Creswellian) tools from Three Holes Cave: 1 trapezoidal backed blade (Cheddar point), 2 scraper on a Magdalenian blade, 3 scraper on blade (2cm scale).

98 Three barbed points of antler from Kent's Cavern.

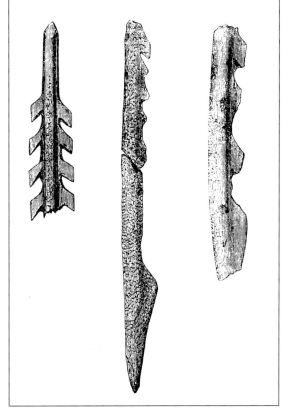

site. Grooves and cuts on pieces of antler and bone indicate how tool blanks were extracted from larger cores using the groove-and-splinter method (see **76**). Among the items of this kind is an exquisite small needle core manufactured from Whooper swan bone, from Gough's Cave.

There are now twenty-eight recognizable Creswellian findspots in England and Wales. Radiocarbon dates on modified bone and antler and human material from these locations provide a remarkably consistent age range of between about 12,600 and 12,000 bp. Although the collections derive mainly from cave sites in the west and mid-central parts of England and Wales, there is increasing evidence for the use of open-air locations in central-north and eastern Britain (**99**).

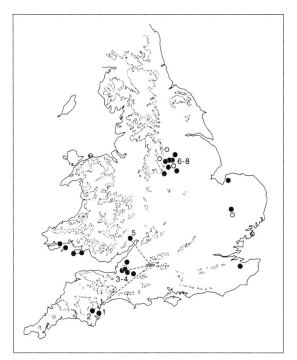

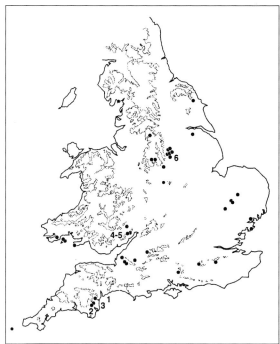

99 Distribution of Creswellian findspots and relationship to flint sources in the Vale of Pewsey. 1 Kent's Cavern, 2 Three Holes Cave, 3–4 Gough's Cave and Sun Hole, 5 King Arthur's Cave, 6–8 Robin Hood's Cave, Pin Hole Cave and Church Hole.

100 Distribution of Final Upper Palaeolithic findspots with penknife points. 1 Pixie's Hole, 2 Broken Cavern, 3 Three Holes Cave, 4–5 King Arthur's Cave and Symond's Yat East, 6 Mother Grundy's Parlour.

In addition to the Creswellian sites there are more than 120 findspots of Final Upper Palaeolithic type (**100** and see **107**). These flint assemblages are distinguished by the occurrence of curve-backed blades and curve-backed points, some with additional basal retouch – known as penknife points (**101**). The points have close affinities with artefacts in German *Federmessergruppen* (literally, 'penknife') assemblages. The dating of this group is so far restricted to a small number of cave sites, but all of them seem to fall within the second half of the interstadial, i.e. after 12,000 bp. The early radiocarbon date from Mother Grundy's Parlour of 11,970 ± 90 bp (on hearth charcoal) suggests there might sometimes be a chronological overlap between the two traditions (Creswellian and Final Upper Palaeolithic). There are a range of direct AMS dates on bone and antler equipment for the second half of the interstadial, which are presumed on grounds of age to be of Final Upper Palaeolithic type.

The only major Final Upper Palaeolithic open-air site so far excavated in Britain is at Hengistbury Head, Dorset. Here excavations conducted by the author in 1981–4 revealed an interesting combination of straight-backed blades and bladelets and large tanged points which have no parallels in Creswellian assemblages.

A later variant of the Final Upper Palaeolithic, characterized by long blades, occupies the end of the Loch Lomond Stadial (after 10,300 bp) and will be dealt with in the final section of this chapter.

Raw materials and mobility

The production of long, slender blades for toolmaking is one of the main characteristics of the Creswellian flint industry. The blades are generally slightly curved in profile and the dorsal scar pattern shows that they were detached from cores with a single preferred flaking direction. Their butts also reveal careful preparation and isolation.

A key requirement in blade-making is selecting the right size and quality of flakeable stone and it is evident that Creswellian people went to some lengths to obtain the best raw material available. In some instances this meant transporting flint many kilometres from its source. We know this from cave sites in Devon which are located in areas where flint is scarce. The blades found at these sites must therefore have been imported from outside the region, perhaps involving distances of 160km (100 miles) (see **100**).

The relationship between raw material sources and sites thus offers a potentially useful signature of Creswellian activity in the Lateglacial. It shows, for example, that flint was either moved or exchanged over relatively long distances. Moreover, rather than carrying whole nodules around the landscape, it is clear that flint was first reduced into more manageable packages of blades before it was transported. This behaviour can be inferred from the absence of the early stages of blade reduction, which are often missing at those sites located well away from flint sources, as at Three Holes Cave (Devon). In other words, only the blades were transported which implies that their makers deliberately travelled light and avoided carrying any extra weight.

101 Final Upper Palaeolithic tools from Pixie's Hole (Devon) and Symond's Yat East (Gloucestershire): 1–2 curve-backed points, 3 angle-backed point, 4 piercer, 5 scraper, 6 burin on truncation, 7 penknife point.

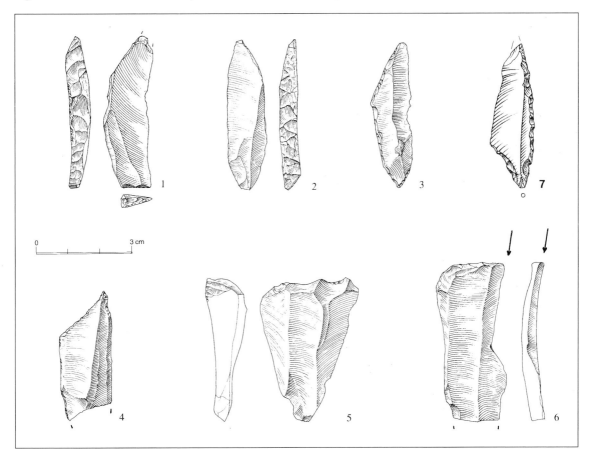

The impression that the Creswellian hunter-gatherers were extremely mobile is also supported by the occurrence of marine shells and other non-local items of North Sea (Baltic) amber found at sites such as Gough's Cave. Similarly, comparison of individual artefacts from caves as far afield as Kent's Cavern (Devon) and Robin Hood Cave (Creswell Crags, Derbyshire) has shown such striking resemblances as to suppose they were made by a single group of people. If confirmed one day by refitting, it would give some approximation of the potential size and geography of the annual range exploited by people in the Lateglacial.

In contrast to the Creswellian, the Final Upper Palaeolithic assemblages are frequently characterized by the use of local raw materials. This is particularly well-illustrated in areas where good quality flint is scarce and where the rocks exploited were in the form of small river cobbles of variable flaking quality. At sites like Pixie's Hole (Devon) the complete reduction sequence is represented from the initial flaking of the pebbles to the manufacture of tools. The retouched tools typically occur on smaller, thicker blades than their equivalents in the Creswellian. One exception to this rule is the site of Hengistbury Head where artefacts are made on relatively long blades. Here, however, it can be argued that the flintknappers were exploiting better than average raw materials, less than 12km (7.5 miles) from the site. As in the example mentioned above, refitting has confirmed that virtually the whole *chaîne opératoire* is represented except for the first few flakes in the reduction sequence (see **colour plates 1** and **2**). Thus, before interpreting raw material behaviour, proper account has to be taken of all of the above factors. The preference for local raw materials by Final Upper Palaeolithic groups may reflect wider changes in the Lateglacial landscape (e.g. increasing forest growth) and these in turn could also have affected mobility.

Seasonality and subsistence

Cut-marks and other signs of modification on bones provide clues about the exploitation of animals by humans and sometimes also reveals when they were hunted. In the Creswellian, faunal species predominantly exploited for meat were wild horse and red deer. At Gough's Cave remains of horse are particularly abundant. Skeletal elements of the head and limb extremities, recorded near the cave entrance, were heavily cut-marked, and showed that the carcasses were probably dismembered and butchered in the daylight, using flint knives. Further into the cave, the recovery of long bone flakes and rib fragments, imply different activities perhaps connected with the smashing and cooking of bone to extract marrow juice and fat. Alternatively, this could have been a rubbish disposal area, with all the activities taking place outside the cave.

By analyzing the nature and location of cut-marks it is often possible to reconstruct the whole butchery process. At Gough's Cave the preparation of the carcasses was extremely thorough and it is clear that little or nothing went to waste. For example, reconstruction shows that after the meat was expertly filleted many of the bones, including jaws, were fractured lengthwise in order to obtain marrow. Even normally meat-poor elements such as the head were not ignored, but were carefully dissected to remove the softer edible tissues of the tongue and brain. The animals were also an important source of raw materials. Skinning marks indicate that the hides were probably valued for making tailored clothing, moccasins or tent covers, while the long bones were potential sources for needle splinters and projectile points. The stripping of carcasses also allowed for the removal of tendons at the back of the legs (for sinew) and the hooves (possibly for reducing to glue) (**102**).

Apart from the food and raw material yield, useful information can also be gained from the teeth and bones concerning seasonality. For example, based on features of tooth eruption it

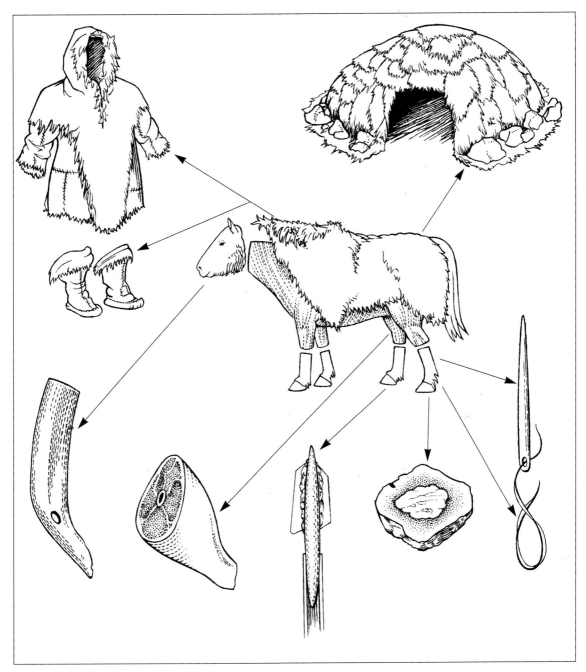

appears that some of the red deer from Gough's Cave were killed in winter or early spring. Other evidence from annual growth bands on the teeth of horse and red deer reveal that the hunting occurred in the summer. This information is important for understanding whether people were present in one area for the whole year or just on a seasonal basis. Gough's Cave would

102 Natural products obtainable from wild horse. Clockwise from top left: parka and boots (coat and hide), tent covering (hide), needle and thread (bone splinters and sinew from backs of legs), glue (hooves), spear tip (bone plus animal glue), meat (especially upper limbs), pendants (horse teeth).

appear to conform to a winter-summer occupation with people moving elsewhere in the autumn, perhaps to the sea coasts where they could fish and trap seals.

One aspect, still largely missing from the British record, are the Creswellian open-air equivalents of cave sites, which might be predicted to occur in the non-limestone areas in the east of the country. So far relatively few findspots of this type are known, but they are likely to include flintwork from Newark (Nottinghamshire), Edlington Wood (Yorkshire), Froggatt (Derbyshire), Lakenheath Warren (Suffolk) and Walton-on-the-Naze (Essex). If these were winter occupation sites then they might be expected to contain evidence of more substantial dwelling structures with post-settings, boiling pits and internal fireplaces. Such structures have indeed been found in the Central German Rhineland at Gönnersdorf where there is clear evidence of winter occupation. On the other hand, if sites were occupied in the autumn and spring they might be expected to resemble more closely open-air locations in the Paris Basin (e.g. Pincevent, Verberie) where tent-like arrangements have been found alongside outdoor hearths with flat stone cooking slabs.

Unfortunately, no well-preserved Upper Palaeolithic living floors have yet been discovered in Britain. However, by implication, large open-air sites like Hengistbury Head probably functioned as major aggregation places where people congregated close to the spring or autumn migration routes of herding animals. Records of uniserial barbed bone and antler points from other parts of the country indicate the preferred types of hunting equipment employed.

Art and symbolism

Despite earlier claims of cave paintings in Britain at Bacon Hole (Gower, West Glamorgan) and in the Wye Valley (Gloucestershire), none has so far proved verifiable. The reason for this absence is hard to explain except in terms of the short-lived, seasonal nature of human settlement patterns, coupled with the presumed low levels of population in Lateglacial Britain.

On the other hand, convincing portable art objects are known from several British Creswellian localities. These include non-figurative abstract engravings on mobiliary items of stone, bone and ivory from Gough's Cave, Robin Hood Cave, Pin Hole (**colour plate 16**) and, possibly, Mother Grundy's Parlour. Church Hole has a unique example of a notched bone pendant. Regularly spaced groups of delicate incisions on hare tibia awls and on a section of bovid rib from Gough's Cave have been variously interpreted as counting tallies, lunar calendars, spacers, message sticks or simply as gaming pieces. Similar notations have been recorded on pieces of mammoth ivory also from Gough's Cave. The only example of figurative art unquestionably connected with the Creswellian is the engraving of a horse on a rib fragment from Robin Hood Cave (**103**), discovered in 1876. A similar example of an engraved horse from Sherbourne (Dorset) has recently been demonstrated to be a skilful forgery.

Examples of mobiliary art of potentially Final Upper Palaeolithic age include four engraved and ochre-stained bone tallies from Kendrick's Cave, Llandudno (north Wales). These items are part of a collection known since the 1880s, which includes a mixture of artefacts and other items of post-Palaeolithic age. Recently one of the tallies has been AMS dated to about 11,800 years ago. The close agreement in age with human bone from the same cave suggests the likelihood of inhumation burials. The only other example of non-figurative artwork from this period is an abstract engraving on the cortex of a refitted flint core from Hengistbury (**104**). Identical incised flints are known from contemporary sites in the Netherlands and France.

The presence of red ochre at Hengistbury, Kendrick's Cave and some of the Creswellian sites indicates the widespread use of this mineral

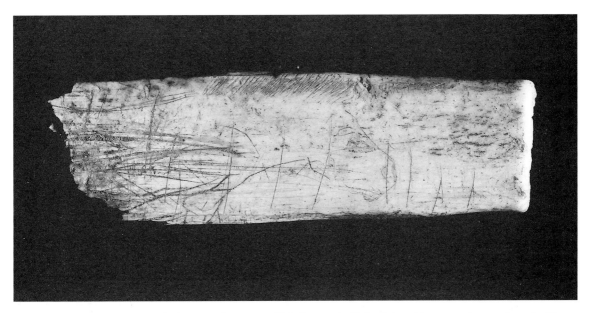

103 Engraving of a horse on a rib fragment from Robin Hood Cave (Derbyshire), discovered in 1876. Length 7.3cm (2.9in).

104 Core and refitting flake with engraved cortex from the Final Upper Palaeolithic site of Hengistbury Head. The refitting flake is about 1cm (0.4in) thick.

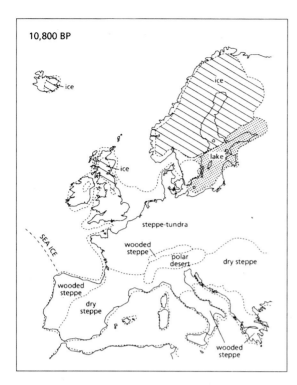

10,800 BP

105 Reconstructed vegetational patterns for the Younger Dryas/Loch Lomond Stadial, around 10,800 bp.

in the Late and Final Upper Palaeolithic. At Hengistbury, ochre fragments and a broken 'crayon' were found in among a concentration of tools including end-scrapers. The co-occurrence of scrapers and red ochre is known from many European Palaeolithic sites where it has often been linked to hideworking activities. Certainly the practical uses of ochre in leather

working (as a vermicide) and for colour decoration are well known in the ethnographic record. The symbolic nature of the blood-red colorant and its widespread use in ritual have also been highlighted in studies of modern hunter-gatherer societies.

Terminal Ice Age

The end of the Interstadial warming cycle did not mark the true finish of the last Ice Age. Evidence from the Greenland ice cores shows a return to much colder stadial conditions in the northern hemisphere between about 10,800 and 10,000 bp. During this phase land temperatures in Britain fell by an estimated 5–7°C and sea pack-ice returned to waters off the north coast of Iberia (**105**). The conditions in Britain were made cooler by the deflection of the warm Gulf Stream currents away from the western European seaboard. Coupled with potentially stronger cyclonic activity in the North Atlantic and a northerly wind flow pattern there seems to have been a net increase in snowfall leading to the regrowth of glaciers in the Scottish Highlands and north Wales (see **21**).

In Britain the much colder conditions of the Loch Lomond Stadial (termed the Younger Dryas Stadial on the Continent) lasted long enough for open-tundra environments to

106 Bruised long blades from Riverdale (Canterbury, Kent) (2cm scale)

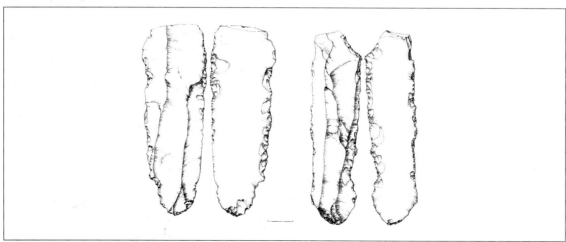

develop and allowed animals like reindeer to return to the British Isles. Other proxy records based on pollen and fossil beetle remains show that the climate also became progressively more arid. There are no reliably dated records of human presence for the coldest part of the Stadial. As in the LGM, it seems that Britain was temporarily abandoned by human groups.

The first sustained evidence of human activity after the cold peak (*c.* 10,500 bp) occurs in southern Britain around 10,200 bp. Lithic artefact assemblages of this period are hard to characterize because of the lack of standardization in the retouched tool equipment. Nevertheless, there does appear to be a fairly consistent pattern in the lithic reduction sequences, which resembles the methods used in the Upper Palaeolithic. The assemblages are generally recognized by very long blades (12cm/5in or more in length) and the presence of blades with distinct battering-damage along their edges (**106**). These 'bruised blades' are believed to be the result of particular activities in which the margins of the blades were used either to chop through materials such as antler or in shaping and replenishing the ends of sandstone hammers. Industries combining long blades and blades with bruised edges have also been recorded from this period in northern Germany and France, where they are attributed to variants of an Ahrensburgian culture.

So far twenty-eight findspots of this type have been discovered in south-east Britain and East Anglia (**107**). Most are located in floodplain or low river valley terrace situations, in places suggesting immediate access to *in situ* geological sources of flint. Where larger scatters of material have been recorded, as at Three Ways Wharf (Uxbridge, Greater London), Sproughton (Suffolk), Riverdale (Kent), Springhead (Kent), Swaffham Prior (Cambridgeshire), Avington VI (Berkshire) and Gatehampton Farm (Oxfordshire) they usually contain a high proportion of blade waste to retouched tools, the latter making up less than 2 per cent of the total assemblage. The absence of hearth

structures and quantities of burnt flints implies only very short-term occupation events. Depending on the accepted interpretation of bruised blades, they may either represent butchery locations (where bone and antler were chopped) or 'knapping floors' (where sandstone hammers were episodically honed). Evidence of the likely age of these sites is given by wild horse remains at Three Ways Wharf which have been dated to 10,270 ± 100 bp.

Several other findspots are thought to be of the same age. They include stray finds of Ahrensburgian tanged points, as at Risby Warren (Humberside), Tayfen Road, Bury St Edmunds (Suffolk) and Doniford Cliff (Somerset). One site, at Avington, contains both points and long blades in among two dense knapping scatters (**108**). Isolated finds of small tanged points have also been made as far north as Orkney in Scotland and, if validated, indicate a much wider geographical distribution

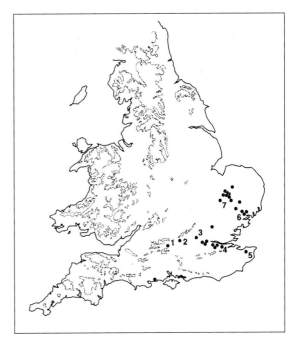

107 Distribution of Final Upper Palaeolithic long blade findspots with bruised blades. 1 Avington VI, 2 Gatehampton, 3 Three Ways Wharf (Uxbridge), 4 Springhead (Lower Floor), 5 Riverdale, 6 Sproughton, 7 Swaffham Prior.

of this Lateglacial technology than hitherto suspected.

Although the organic components of these sites are frequently missing, one site in Germany has yielded some sensational organic artefacts. The find was made by Alfred Rust at Stellmoor (the original type-site of the Ahrensburgian), near Hamburg, where flint finds identical to the British ones were recovered on the eve of the Second World War. The site was situated near the edge of a former lake in one of the steep-sided Ahrensburg tunnel valleys which criss-cross this part of the North German Plain. At the end of the last ice age the movements of migrating

herds of reindeer were probably channelled along these valleys and at Stellmoor a mass concentration of about 18,000 reindeer bones were found in the lake muds. Many of the bones had lesions and impact wounds, which in a few cases, contained flint points actually embedded inside them. According to seasonal indicators the animals were probably killed in the autumn. In among the concentration of bone and antler were the spectacular remains of 105 pinewood arrowshafts, some preserved with their small tanged flint tips still intact (**109** and **110**). The existence of archery equipment in the Lateglacial had long been suspected but this was the first

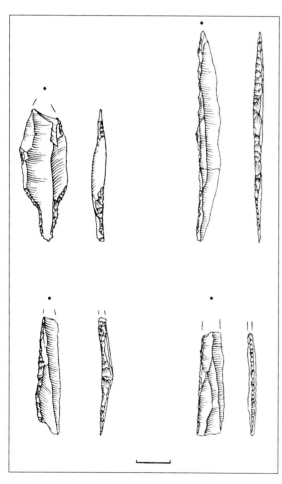

108 Final Upper Palaeolithic long blade tools from Avington VI (Berkshire). Top left, clockwise: Ahrensburgian tanged point, backed bi-point, backed blade, oblique point (1cm scale).

109 Pinewood arrowshafts from Stellmoor. The arrows consisted of two parts: a main shaft and a foreshaft. The foreshafts were expertly designed to break away from the mainshaft leaving the arrowhead firmly embedded in the animal. The loose mainshaft could then be retrieved and respliced with a new flint-tipped foreshaft.

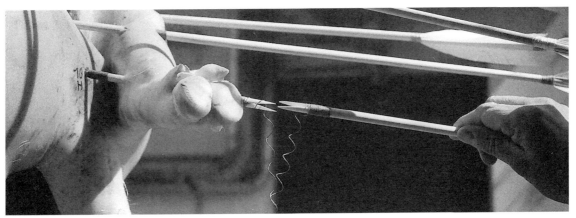

110 Experimentally reconstructed arrowshafts from Stellmoor showing how the foreshaft and mainshaft separate.

time that preservation conditions had allowed the survival of such ancient hunting implements. Although all of these breathtaking artefacts were destroyed in the war, an excellent photographic record of them still exists. Apart from the arrowshafts the ends of two wooden bows were also recovered. The bows, made in one piece of fir, would have made extremely powerful hunting weapons, equally well-suited for driving and ambushing or for individual stalking.

While there is no direct proof of contemporary reindeer hunting in Britain there is certainly good evidence that these animals were present in the Loch Lomond Stadial. Indeed the archaeologist Roger Jacobi has postulated that the Lateglacial reindeer migration routes could easily have traversed the dry North Sea Plain (**111**). Based on the present-day annual lifecycle of these animals, it is known that pregnant reindeer cows will often choose high rocky barren areas well away from predators in order to calve. The movement of cows towards the calving grounds, accompanied by juveniles, usually begins in spring and it is feasible that the rugged upland interior of Britain served as a safe haven for birthing. After the resumption of herd activity on the summer feeding grounds (perhaps on the North Sea lowlands), the autumn migration trails may have led the animals along the German tunnel valleys to the winter refuges south of the treeline.

Although no supporting evidence yet exists to support this theory it is interesting that one of the largest assemblages of reindeer remains of

Loch Lomond Stadial age comes from Ossum's Cave in the Manifold Valley (Staffordshire). The assemblage has been interpreted as marking a likely wolf kill and it is notable for the fact that it contains juvenile animals. Indeed Kate Scott, who has analyzed the fauna, has demonstrated that the majority of animals died in spring. Despite the absence of clear signs of human interference with the bones, there are some associated flints which could be contemporary. It is intriguing to think that human groups occupying Britain in spring may have followed the reindeer herds all the way back across the North Sea Plains, continuing to exploit them in the autumn.

Parallels to the British 'long blade' assemblages have also been described from the Somme Valley (northern France) and the Paris Basin, although so far not in combination with the characteristic tanged flint points. Where bone is preserved at these sites, it seems to be associated with either wild horse or bovids, rather than reindeer. Four AMS dates on horse teeth from the site of Belloy-sur-Somme in Picardy range from $10,260 \pm 160$ bp to $9,720 \pm 130$ bp and overlap in age with Three Ways Wharf.

An interesting group of decorated objects of this period, but with no demonstrable flint associations, has been recovered from Kendrick's Cave, Llandudno. They comprise a

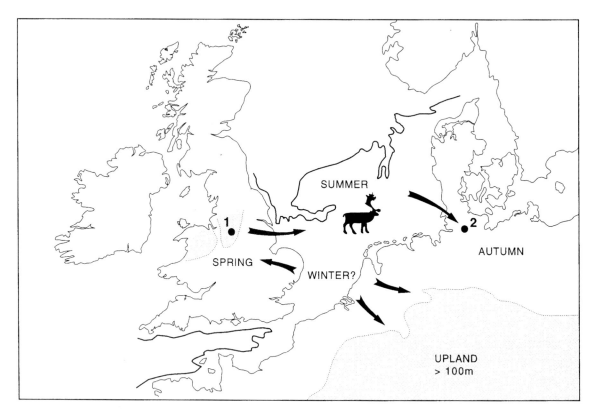

111 Possible reindeer migration routes in the Loch Lomond Stadial. 1=Ossum's Cave 2=Stellmoor.

112 Decorated horse jaw with incised chevrons from Kendrick's Cave (north Wales).

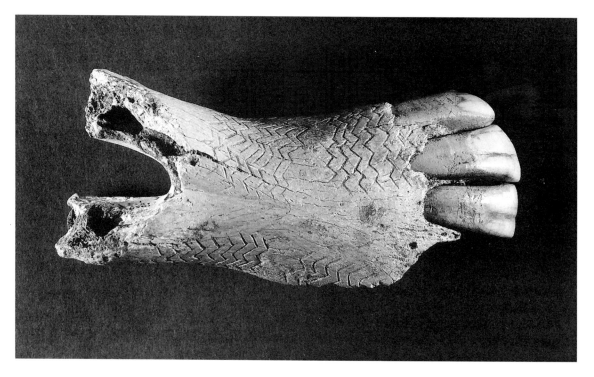

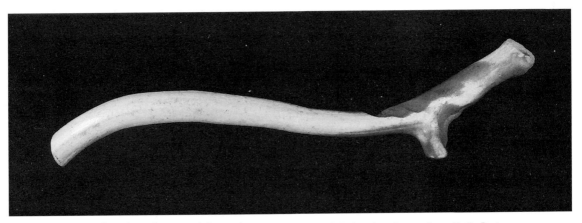

113 Reindeer Lyngby axe from Earl's Barton (Northamptonshire)

horse jaw incised with a chevron (zig-zag) design (**112**) and perforated and decorated badger and deer teeth beads. According to new radiocarbon dates all of these items are just over 10,000 years old. While some doubts still exist over the original context of these finds, they do seem to form a coherent series of art objects which may once have been associated with a human burial. The only other directly dated object in this period is a 'Lyngby axe' (a reindeer antler club) which was recovered at Earl's Barton (Northamptonshire) and has an age of 10,320 ± 150 bp (**113**).

In this chapter we have considered the occupation of Britain at the end of the last glaciation. Following a major gap in settlement coinciding with the LGM, relatively warm interstadial conditions permitted the recolonization of Britain after about 12,600 bp. During this period humans left a distinctive set of archaeological signatures in caves and open-air sites. The associated animal remains reflect temperate environments and notably exclude cold climatic indicators such as reindeer. The interstadial was followed by a return to intensely cold conditions in the Loch Lomond Stadial when reindeer reappeared in the native fauna. People seemed once again to have been absent, but towards the end of this cold phase hunter-gatherers with a developed bow-hunting technology returned, probably to exploit reindeer and wild horse.

To conclude, the end of the Loch Lomond/Younger Dryas cold stadial is signalled by a dramatic post-glacial climatic warming across Britain and western Europe. The impact of such changes on people and the environment must have been enormous, not least because of the astonishing rapidity with which these occurred. According to some estimates the climatic transition may have taken place over as little as ten to fifty years; in other words, well within a normal human lifespan. Temperatures at the onset of the postglacial (c. 10,000 bp) seem to have risen to at least as high as those of the present day. At the same time the archaeological record is characterized by new Mesolithic industries containing items of specialist woodworking equipment (transversely sharpened axes and adzes), presumably reflecting the increasingly wooded nature of the environment. It is noteworthy, however, that some of the microlith projectile types found in the Early Mesolithic are virtually identical to Latest Palaeolithic examples (see **108**), implying that division of these groupings may be somewhat arbitrary. Thus the end of the Palaeolithic, the main subject of this book, is not marked by a complete break in cultural traditions. Instead, we find evidence of technological continuity and only gradual economic change. Indeed, it was not until around 5,000 years later that the lifestyles of indigenous hunter-gatherers were once and for all eclipsed by the advent of farming.

Glossary

AMS Accelerator Mass Spectrometry or AMS dating refers to the method used for measuring very small amounts of ^{14}C (necessary for radiocarbon dating). The charged particles are detected by subjecting them to strong magnetic fields in a tandem accelerator.

barbed point or harpoon The difference between these two implements is that the harpoon generally exhibits a tang or hole at one end for the attachment of a line. Uniserial points (barbs along one edge) of bone and antler occur in the British Late Upper Palaeolithic, and are more common than biserial examples.

bifacial A term used to describe a stone tool shaped on both faces, as in a handaxe.

blade A long narrow flake with parallel edges, usually with a length to width ratio of more than 2:1, and struck from a specially prepared core. In Europe, the earliest blades and blade tools are generally associated with the Upper Palaeolithic.

bladelet Traditionally, a bladelet is a blade less than 12mm (0.5in) wide, but in the case of tools such as backed bladelets, it refers to artefacts narrower than 9mm (0.3in).

bp Before the present, i.e. before AD 1950. Conventionally, radiocarbon dates are expressed in years bp, whereas dates obtained by other methods use calendrical years (and are often expressed in years bc). The term 'years ago' is used to denote ages beyond the accepted ^{14}C time range (about 50,000 years).

burin A tool with a chisel-like edge made by striking a thin spall down the side of a flake or blade. It is often associated with the carving of bone, antler and ivory equipment (e.g. harpoons and spear tips) but use-wear analysis shows these tools were also used for scraping purposes.

core A lump of stone used as parent material for making flakes and blades.

flake A stone artefact whose length is less than twice its width.

glacial maximum The peak of an ice age when ice sheets are at their greatest extent and temperatures at their lowest. The LGM (Last Glacial Maximum) can be dated in Europe to about 18,000 bp.

haft The handle part of an implement such as an axe or knife. Upper Palaeolithic examples are usually made of antler, bone or ivory.

Holocene The present geological epoch, which began about 10,000 bp.

hominid A member of the family *Hominidae* which includes both extinct and modern forms of human.

interglacial A warm interval between periods of glaciation characterized by temperatures at least as high as those of today and consequently by reduced ice cover.

interstadial A short-lived period of warmer temperatures in a glacial phase, lasting anywhere from between about 50 and 2000 years.

isothermic line A line on a map linking places of equal temperature at a given time.

microwear analysis *see* use-wear analysis

mobiliary art Decorated artefacts of stone, bone, ivory, etc which were small enough to be carried from site to site, e.g. statuettes, figurines and pendants; cf parietal art.

palaeoanthropology The study of prehistoric humans as revealed by fossil remains.

Palaeolithic Literally the 'Old Stone Age' which began about 2.5 million years ago with the emergence of toolmakers and continued until the end of the Pleistocene about 10,000 years ago.

parietal art Art, usually paintings, on rock walls at cave sites.

periglacial The term used for both the climate and characteristic cold-climate landforms and sediments found in areas adjacent to ice sheets.

Pleistocene The first interval of the geological period known as the Quaternary, and preceding the present epoch or Holocene in which we all live. Various estimates place the beginning of the Pleistocene at either 2.5 million years ago or about 1.8 million years ago.

pseudofacts/pseudoartefacts Natural objects which take the form of artefacts.

retouch A term which describes the secondary modification of a blade or flake by percussion or pressure flaking, as in making a scraper or burin.

scraper A tool usually consisting of a convex (semi-circular) edge which has been modified by retouch. Scrapers were used to prepare animal hides and to shape wood, antler, bone and ivory artefacts.

tang A long, slender projecting strip or prong of a tool, often fitted into a handle or shaft.

use-wear analysis The study of stone tool surfaces for signs of alteration due to use. Sometimes referred to as microwear analysis, the alterations may occur in the form of micro-polishes and striations usually only visible under the microscope. By comparing the ancient use-wear with that found on experimentally generated examples it is possible to determine past tool use.

Places to visit

Museums with Palaeolithic artefacts and Pleistocene mammal collections

Bolton Museum and Art Gallery, Le Mans Crescent, Bolton, Lancashire BL1 1SE
Upper Palaeolithic collections and fauna

British Museum, Bloomsbury, London, WC1B 3DG
Galleries currently undergoing reorganization, major holdings of British and European material in the Quaternary Section at Franks House

Buxton Museum and Art Gallery, Terrace Road, Buxton, Derbyshire SK17 6DU
Manifold Valley Upper Palaeolithic and fauna

Castle Museum, Norwich, Norfolk NR1 3JU
Lower Palaeolithic, some Upper Palaeolithic plus Quaternary mammals

Cheddar Show Caves Museum, Cheddar Gorge, Cheddar, Somerset BS27 3QF
Late Upper Palaeolithic finds and fauna from the Cheddar caves

City of Bristol Museum and Art Gallery, Queen's Road, Bristol BS1 1VE
Middle and Upper Palaeolithic collections

Derby Museum and Art Gallery, The Strand, Derby DE1 1BS
Upper Palaeolithic collections and fauna

Ipswich Museum, High Street, Ipswich, Suffolk IP1 3QH
Recently updated Palaeolithic exhibition

Jersey Museum, 9 Pier Road, St Helier, Jersey, Channel Islands
Middle Palaeolithic material from La Cotte

Lancaster Museum, Market Square, Lancaster, Lancashire LA1 1HT
Upper Palaeolithic collections from north-west England

Liverpool Museum, William Brown Street, Liverpool L3 8EN
Kent's Cavern and Quaternary collections

The Manchester Museum, University of Manchester, Oxford Road, Manchester M13 9PL
Creswell Crags Middle and Upper Palaeolithic holdings, large collection of Pleistocene mammals

National Museum of Wales, Cathays Park, Cardiff, South Glamorgan CF1 3NP
General displays of Palaeolithic sites from Wales

Newark Museum, Appletongate, Newark, Nottinghamshire NG24 1JY
Lower Palaeolithic material

Oxford University Museum, Parks Road
Red Lady of Paviland plus artefacts and fauna

Pitt Rivers Museum, Parks Road, Oxford OX1 3PP
Mainly ethnographic material but prehistoric Old World collections displayed in the nearby Balfour Building at 60 Banbury Road

Sheffield City Museum, Weston Park, Sheffield S10 2TP

Lower and Upper Palaeolithic collections

Taunton Museum, The Castle, Castle Green, Taunton, Somerset TA1 4AA

Important Pleistocene mammals collection and display

Tenby Museum, Castle Hill, Tenby, Pembrokeshire SA70 7BP

Upper Palaeolithic collections from sites in south-west Wales

Torquay Natural History Society Museum, Babbacombe Road, Torquay TQ1 1HG

Lower, Middle and Upper Palaeolithic finds and fauna from Kent's Cavern

Wells Museum, 8 Cathedral Green, Wells, Somerset BA5 2UE

Middle Palaeolithic material from Somerset Caves

Show caves open to the public

Creswell Crags Caves and Visitors Centre, Crags Road, Welbeck, Worksop, Nottinghamshire S80 3LH

Small collection of artefacts and replicas from Creswell, pedestrian access to sites with guide. Caves are gated.

Gough's Cave, Cheddar Gorge, Cheddar, Somerset BS27 3QF

Guides available

Kent's Cavern, Wellswood, Torquay, Devon TQ1 2JS

Guided tour

Wookey Hole Cave (and Hyaena Den), Wells, Somerset BA5 1BB

Guided tour

Caves and open-air sites with public access

Aveline's Hole, Burrington Combe, Somerset (ST 476587)

Entrance on a sharp bend of the B3134 in the Mendip Hills. No information available at the site.

Cathole, Parkmill, West Glamorgan (SS 538900)

Set in parkland on the Gower near the famous Parc le Breos chambered tomb. No information available at the site.

Hengistbury Head, Bournemouth, Dorset (SZ 179906)

Overlooking the Solent on the south side of the headland. New interpretation centre being planned. There is a site guide and a marked pedestrian route.

Hoyle's Mouth, Penally, Pembrokeshire (SN 112003)

No information available at the site

King Arthur's Cave, Whitchurch, Herefordshire (SO 546156)

Scenic location overlooking the River Wye in the Forest of Dean. No information available at the site.

Swanscombe, Barnfield Pit, Dartford, Kent (TQ 598743)

Information available at leisure centre next to the site

Victoria Cave, Settle, North Yorkshire (SD 838650)

Located in the spectacular limestone countryside of the Yorkshire Dales. No information available at the site.

Further reading

Bahn, Paul and Jean Vertut 1988, *Images of the Ice Age*, Windward.

Barton, Nicholas, Alison Roberts and Derek Roe (eds) 1991, *The Late Glacial in NW Europe*, Council for British Archaeology, Research Report 77, London.

Dennell, Robin 1983, *European Economic Prehistory. A New Approach*, Academic Press, London.

Gamble, Clive 1993, *Timewalkers*, Penguin.

Gowlett, John 1992, *Ascent to Civilisation* (2nd edn), McGraw-Hill.

Green, Stephen and Elizabeth Walker 1991, *Ice Age Hunters: Neanderthals and Early Modern Hunters in Wales*, National Museum of Wales, Cardiff.

Johanson, Donald and Blake Edgar 1996, *From Lucy to Language*, Weidenfeld and Nicholson.

Jones, R, and David Keen 1993, *Pleistocene Environments in the British Isles*. Chapman and Hall, London.

Lawson, Andrew 1991, *Cave Art*, Shire, Princes Risborough.

Lister, Adrian and Paul Bahn 1995, *Mammoths*, Boxtree, London.

Lord, John 1993, *The Nature and Subsequent Uses of Flint. Vol 1. The basics of lithic technology*, John Lord, Brandon.

Lowe, John and Michael Walker, 1997, *Reconstructing Quaternary Environments*, Longman.

Mellars, Paul 1996, *The Neanderthal Legacy*, Princeton University Press.

Mithen, Steven 1996, *The Prehistory of the Mind*, Thames and Hudson.

Pitts, Michael and Mark Roberts, 1997, *Fairweather Eden*, Century.

Roe, Derek 1981, *The Lower and Middle Palaeolithic Periods in Britain*, Routledge & Kegan Paul.

Smith, Christopher 1992, *Late Stone Age Hunters of the British Isles*, Routledge.

Stringer, Chris and Clive Gamble 1993, *In Search of the Neanderthals*, Thames & Hudson.

Stringer, Chris and Robin McKie 1996, *African Exodus: The Origins of Modern Humanity*, Jonathan Cape, London.

Stuart, Anthony 1988, *Life in the Ice Age*, Shire Books, Princes Risborough.

Tattersall, Ian 1995, *The Last Neanderthal*, Macmillan, USA.

Tattersall, Ian 1995, *The Fossil Trail*, Oxford University Press.

Trinkaus, Erik and Pat Shipman, 1993, *The Neanderthals: Changing the Image of Mankind*, Jonathan Cape, London.

Wymer, J. J. 1982. *The Palaeolithic Age*, Croom Helm, Kent.

Index

The Author

Dr Nicholas Barton is senior lecturer in the Department of Anthropology at Oxford Brookes University. He previously worked at the University of Wales (Lampeter) and as an Inspector of Ancient Monuments for English Heritage. His main areas of research are Palaeolithic and Mesolithic archaeology. He has directed excavations at Hengistbury Head, Dorset, and in the Torbryan Valley, Devon (with Alison Roberts). He is currently engaged in a landscape study of caves in the Wye Valley, Herefordshire, and is co-director, with Professor Chris Stringer, of the Gibraltar Caves Project.

'One of the great classic series of British archaeology.' *Current Archaeology*

This volume is part of a major series, jointly conceived for English Heritage and Batsford, under the general editorship of Dr Stephen Johnson at English Heritage.

Titles in the series:

Sites
Avebury Caroline Malone
Danebury Barry Cunliffe
Dover Castle Jonathan Coad
Flag Fen: Prehistoric Fenland Centre Francis Pryor
Fountains Abbey Glyn Coppack
Glastonbury Philip Rahtz
Hadrian's Wall Stephen Johnson
Housesteads James Crow
Ironbridge Gorge Catherine Clark
Lindisfarne Deirdre O'Sullivan and Robert Young
Maiden Castle Niall M. Sharples
Roman Bath Barry Cunliffe
Roman London Gustav Milne
Roman York Patrick Ottaway
St Augustine's Abbey, Canterbury Richard Gem et al.
Stonehenge Julian Richards
Tintagel Charles Thomas
The Tower of London Geoffrey Parnell
Viking Age York Richard Hall
Wharram Percy: Deserted Medieval Village Maurice Beresford and John Hurst

Periods
Anglo-Saxon England Martin Welch
Bronze Age Britain Michael Parker Pearson
Industrial England Michael Stratton and Barrie Trinder
Iron Age Britain Barry Cunliffe
Norman England Trevor Rowley
Roman Britain Martin Millett
Stone Age Britain Nicholas Barton
Viking Age England Julian D. Richards

Subjects
Abbeys and Priories Glyn Coppack
Canals Nigel Crowe
Castles Tom McNeill
Channel Defences Andrew Saunders
Church Archaeology Warwick Rodwell
Life in Roman Britain Joan Alcock
Prehistoric Settlements Robert Bewley
Roman Forts in Britain Paul Bidwell
Roman Towns in Britain Guy de la Bédoyère
Roman Villas and the Countryside Guy de la Bédoyère
Ships and Shipwrecks Peter Marsden
Shrines and Sacrifice Ann Woodward
Victorian Churches James Stevens Curl

Towns
Canterbury Marjorie Lyle
Chester Peter Carrington
Durham Martin Roberts
Norwich Brian Ayers
Winchester Tom Beaumont James
York Richard Hall

Landscapes through Time
Dartmoor Sandy Gerrard
Peak District John Barnatt and Ken Smith
Yorkshire Dales Robert White
Forthcoming
Lake District Robert Bewley